Rigby
INFOQUEST

Grade
5

TEACHER'S RESOURCE

Rigby.

Contents

Student Books Overview and Notes 36

About *Rigby InfoQuest*

Rigby InfoQuest is a nonfiction series of resources for enhancing literacy development and learning across your class's curriculum. Current research and curriculum developments have highlighted the need for students to develop visual literacy and critical thinking skills in addition to the decoding and text processing skills associated with learning to read. It is becoming increasingly important for students to become self-directed learners who can logically research and then coherently present information. *Rigby InfoQuest's* rich components provide many opportunities for introducing these crucial skills, inviting engaged practice, and encouraging students' extension of their learning.

This Teacher's Resource

On the following pages you will find ideas and activities for guiding your students' reading of the nonfiction materials in the series so they will also have a better understanding of other nonfiction texts and visuals that they need to use in the world. The suggestions provide a variety of ways that you can flexibly best support your students' learning based on their needs. Included in this Teacher's Resource are blackline masters for comprehension practice and assessment.

InfoMagazines

There are 2 InfoMagazines for each grade level 5 and 6. These engage students as you introduce nonfiction organization or features, demonstrate skill use, and share curriculum content in a group or whole-class setting. You will find helpful, specific suggestions for using the InfoMagazines in this Teacher's Resource on pages 28–35.

The InfoMagazines can be used for a variety of purposes, including introducing students to the special content features, text organizers, and visual literacy elements they will meet in the Student Books.

Each InfoMagazine offers a range of possible teaching points. Suggestions for informal assessment of each of these teaching points are included in the InfoMagazine notes. The outcomes of the informal assessment can be used to help select Student Books that feature elements to be taught, consolidated, or further explored. (See the Student Book Overview on pp. 36–39.) The InfoMagazine notes also include 2 blackline masters that encourage critical thinking skills.

Student Books

There are 20 different Student Books for each grade level 3–6 catering to ages 8–11. Each grade is color coded: grade 3 is orange, grade 4 is green, grade 5 is blue, and grade 6 is purple. The books supplement each grade's curriculum and content area requirements. These Student Books contain:

- manageable main text leveled for the age group's average reading ability.
- text organizers, including tables of content, headings, subheadings, bullets, captions, labels, indexes, glossaries, and bibliographies.
- visual elements so students interpret diagrams, cutaways, cross sections, maps, keys, tables, graphs, charts, and time lines.

Please see pages 36–119 of this Teacher's Resource for book-specific suggestions.

www.rigbyinfoquest.com

Each Student Book has its own specially designed Web site pages, with text leveled to match the Student Book. Two activities are provided on the Web site for each Student Book.

Using the *Rigby InfoQuest* Web Site

Your students will log on to the secure "Siteseeing" Web site at **www.rigbyinfoquest.com** to delve further into a topic from each Student Book. They can find information to answer research questions, which are provided for you on pages 41–117 of this Teacher's Resource, and they can also complete extension activities. The site can be ideal for classroom use or homework.

Teacher Registration

It is best to go to **www.rigbyinfoquest.com** using the *Internet Explorer* browser. This site uses Flash software; an onscreen prompt will identify if your computer has the correct software or not. If your computer does not have it, simply follow the hyperlink to freely download Flash.

Set up an individual user name for each student. To allocate these user names, click the "Teacher Log In" button. This brings up a screen on which you can create and maintain a class list. [Note: As you fill in the fields, there is a space for your ZIP code. You must fill this in. If you do not have a ZIP code, insert any number so you can continue. If you are uncertain about what to do at any point, the Help button can provide information.]

Follow the registration process. Click the "Register" button and type in the fields. When you have completed all the fields, click the "Register" button at the bottom of the page. You will be directed to a student registration page. Here, enter each student's name and grade level of work. This will automatically generate a user name for each student.

Student List		
Student	**User Name**	**Grade/Year**
Charlotte Michaels	CharlotteM	Grade 5
Dylan Smith	DylanS	Grade 5
Mike Egmont	MikeE	Grade 5
Samantha Duffy	SamanthaD	Grade 5
Tara Ryan	TaraR	Grade 5

Click here for a version of the student list you can print

The grade that is selected for students will determine whether they access the Grade 3, 4, 5, or 6 section of the Web site when they log in with their user names. The information you enter will be displayed as a printable list.

Student Log In

A student logging in simply goes to **www.rigbyinfoquest.com**, clicks the "Student Log In" button, and enters her or his user name in the provided field. The Siteseeing main page will next appear so the student can begin work.

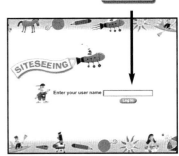

Site Navigation

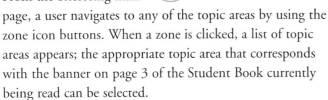

From the Siteseeing main page, a user navigates to any of the topic areas by using the zone icon buttons. When a zone is clicked, a list of topic areas appears; the appropriate topic area that corresponds with the banner on page 3 of the Student Book currently being read can be selected.

- A student navigates through the reading pages of the selected topic area and logs out by using the clickable bar located in the top right corner of each page. If there is ever a problem loading a complete page, the page button in the bar can be clicked to refresh the content.

- Red text signifies that a box with additional information is available. Blue text signifies that a dictionary definition is available. The student clicks on the text to link to the information.

- When the cursor is moved over an image and the symbol changes from an arrow to a hand, it signifies that an information box is available from the image. The student clicks anywhere on the image to link to the information.

The activities for a topic area can be accessed from Page 4. The "Click here" button brings an activity onscreen. Writing activities can be completed onscreen, and all activities can be printed when they are completed.

When any activity has been completed, the student should click the "Log out" button to record that the activity is completed. This will record on the class list that the student has completed an activity for the Student Book.

Students can navigate to a different zone at any time. They can do this from all the topic areas by clicking one of the banner icons along the left side of any reading page.

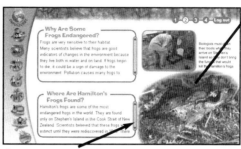

ARROWS TO SCROLL THROUGH TEXT

KEYBOARD PRINTING INSTRUCTIONS

LOG OUT BUTTON

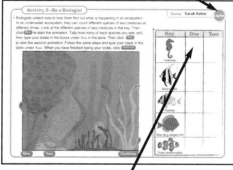

TEXT CAN BE TYPED ONSCREEN

BANNER ICONS

Special Content Features

Every book in *Rigby InfoQuest* contains several special features to extend or challenge students' reading and thinking about extra information. At the Grade 5 level, these are…

Interesting information about the origins and meanings of words

Word Builders can be used to broaden vocabulary and the understanding of how words work.

Procedural text

Students are given opportunities to read and follow sets of instructions and create anything from a Berlese funnel to banana poi.

Detailed, behind-the-scenes close-ups

This information takes students deeper into topics but is not more complex text.

Interesting historical facts

Time Link can lead students to consider what they are learning in a broader context.

Tips and fascinating facts about inventions and development

Students can relate what they are reading to real-life applications.

Biographical information

Famous people, their careers, and their achievements over challenges are the focus.

Newspaper reports, interviews, and magazine articles

Students are encouraged to connect what they are studying with what is happening in the world.

Snippets of useful, intriguing information

These facts increase general knowledge and can be the basis of further research.

Information related to environmental issues

Earth Watch can help students focus on contemporary environmental issues.

Presentation of both sides of an issue

Students are given the opportunity to form and justify opinions about a range of issues.

Narrative text in a diary format

Students can read personal diary entries written by a variety of people.

Questions directly related to text and illustrations

Students can search text and illustrations for specific information.

Information, research ideas, and interesting activities

Students explore this safe Web site to build research skills, learn, and demonstrate their learning for assessment or evaluation.

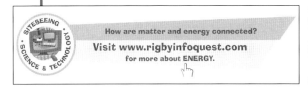

Research Starters
Challenging Questions

Research Starters can be used before reading a book to introduce topics, encourage research, and access students' interest and prior knowledge, or they can be used after reading the book to generate further research and discussions.

Nonfiction Text in the Classroom

Considering Genre Differences

Nonfiction text differs from fictional material in significant ways.

- Nonfiction text has more text organizers, more visual literacy elements, and often a variety of genre.
- Usually, nonfiction material does not need to be read from front to back.
- Perhaps the most important difference is that the learning outcome goals that are planned for reading nonfiction material are quite different from those for fictional material.

Choosing Learning Outcomes

The learning outcomes planned for fictional text often focus on the process of reading. For example, goals may be set so students build their abilities to

- monitor their own reading.
- use appropriate reading strategies.
- self-correct when meaning breaks down.
- read with fluency and expression.
- comprehend a story.

While the learning outcome goals for nonfiction text certainly include these reading process skills, there are critical thinking skills that are highly important for successful comprehension of nonfiction material. These include:

- recognizing important information
- forming generalizations
- evaluating fact and opinion
- comparing and contrasting
- sequencing and summarizing
- classifying, categorizing, and organizing
- interpreting maps and diagrams
- judging validity of information
- identifying cause, effect, and consequences.

In general, it is the ability to use these critical thinking skills that students need to develop as they move from *learning to read* to *reading to learn*.

Thinking About Readability

The perception of students' reading materials needing to be at specific reading levels sometimes precludes teachers from using nonfiction in their literacy teaching. They may be unsure of texts' reading levels. The readability level of any text is influenced by a range of factors.

The Readers's Background Knowledge

What readers bring to a text strongly influences their abilities to comprehend it. To some extent, teachers can build background knowledge before students read texts.

The Vocabulary

Simple words don't necessarily make a book easier to read. In nonfiction texts, the glossary can be used to familiarize students with unfamiliar and technical vocabulary.

The Text Structure and Sentence Complexity

The way information is organized, presented, and illustrated is an important consideration in making texts accessible to young readers. Teachers can help students by teaching about characteristics of common organization in nonfiction texts such as headings, subheadings, labels, captions, body copy, contents, indexes, and glossaries.

The Cohesiveness and Coherence of the Text

When selecting nonfiction texts, consider what the text requires of each reader and what the reader brings to the text. The factors that influence readability levels of nonfiction texts can be manipulated by the teacher, thus making a wide range of books accessible for the majority of the class.

The body copy of the books and Web site in the *Rigby InfoQuest* series is at the average grade level (Grade Three, age 8 years; Grade Four, age 9 years; Grade Five, age 10 years; Grade Six, age 11 years). Each grade's texts have been trialed with the age group for which they are intended. They are suited for a guided reading approach with most students in an age group, resulting in students' 90–95% accuracy when reading the text. The special content features in the books usually contain more challenging text. These may require a shared or reading aloud approach.

Planning for Success

The following steps are useful for planning the reading of nonfiction material.

1. **Decide what the learning outcome(s) will be for the reading.**

   Based on the needs of the students and the content of the selected text, choose one or more learning outcomes for students to achieve.

2. **Set purpose(s) for reading.**

   Before the reading, you will clarify with your students what the purposes are and what they will learn.

3. **If you will be guiding students' reading, plan questions and activities.**

   These questions and activities will support students to achieve the learning outcomes.

4. **Plan how you or students will model responses to the text and visual elements.**

   The modeling will demonstrate how to use information related to the learning outcomes, and the information can be recorded using an appropriate format.

5. **Prepare for responding and appropriately extending learning.**

   Students may complete what has been modeled and use what has been learned in different ways.

6. **Decide how you or students will assess their reading and thinking.**

   Assessment should be focused on the learning outcomes.

Using *Rigby InfoQuest*

Choosing Texts

To broaden understanding of topics, genre, text organizers, and visual elements, there are choices for comprehensive reading experiences. The overviews on pages 36–39 will help you to quickly locate related books for your choice.

1. The whole or part of an InfoMagazine may be initially read or later reread to introduce, clarify, or extend what is met in a Student Book or other curriculum studies. Then more Student Books with related content can be read.

2. Select books around a general topic. Work through these, using the appropriate teaching approach with groups of students or your whole class.

3. Groups of students at the same or different reading levels may wish to form interest groups, select books to read, and then discuss what they've read for curriculum related or recreational reading purposes. The main role for you is to help the students select appropriate material and then ensure the students who need support are receiving it, either from you or from other students. Remember the Web site offers research questions that broaden book topics and suggests other connected Student Book reading.

Choosing Approaches to the Texts

There are flexible ways you can use the texts with your students and teach with this resource. Your knowledge of the needs and capabilities of the students and the requirements of the curriculum will help determine which approaches will be appropriate.

There will be times when it is important for the whole class to gain specific content from a particular text. You can make any book in *Rigby InfoQuest* a successful reading experience for all students by altering the teaching approach.

The choosing of an approach is the major way of controlling text difficulty. Whether working with an individual student, a small group, or the whole class, you can choose one or a combination of the approaches.

- For the first reading of an InfoMagazine and with students who may find a Student Book's text overly challenging, the approach can be a combination of *reading aloud* and *shared reading*.
- With students reading slightly below the level of a text, *shared* and *guided reading* can be used.
- With students reading at or slightly above the level of a text, the approach can be *guided* and some *independent reading*.
- For students reading well above the level of a text, you may choose to set research questions and have the students read the text *independently*.

Reading Aloud

When passages of text are overly challenging for students, the first reading can be one of your reading to them. This enables students to concentrate on the meaning of the passages. A conversation about the text should be shared before and following the reading. The discussion will support and help develop the students' fuller understanding of the text.

Shared Reading

You may wish to highlight information that is unfamiliar to students. Reading these passages with your students enables you to focus on specific detail while maintaining student involvement. It is often useful to use oral cloze, withdrawing your voice on words or phrases that students can manage or when you wish to observe the students' attempts. As in reading aloud, there is also a conversation about the text.

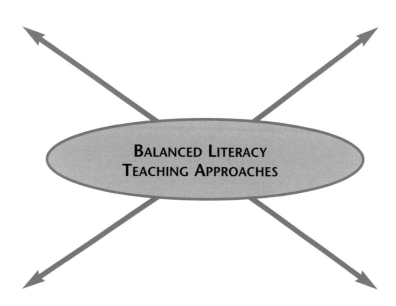

BALANCED LITERACY
TEACHING APPROACHES

Guided Reading

When text material is at an appropriate level of challenge, you can preview and ask questions to guide students' focus on their reading. As students read silently, you can observe the strategies they are using to process the text and understand the information. Support is given individually when it is required. It is important during previewing and questioning to use the vocabulary that students will meet in the text.

Paired and Independent Reading

You may wish to combine more capable students with those needing support. Although this needs to be carefully monitored, there are often benefits for both students. Questions can be posed that focus the students' research reading. When the text to be read is well within students' capabilities, a passage, a page, or even the whole text can be assigned to be read independently.

Tips for Teaching Text Organizers

Text organizers abound in informational text, and students need to understand them to be successful readers and writers. The following are suggestions for procedures that can be applied to many texts.

Tables of Contents

- Turn to a contents page. Discuss the placement of text and page numbers. Have students practice quickly turning to an appropriate page. For example, using the *People of the Pacific Rim* Student Book, ask *Can you find the section about life on the Rim? Which comes first—"Schools on the Rim" or "On the Move"?*
- Discuss the author's decision to arrange the text in the order seen on the contents page. Ask questions such as *Why do you think the section "The Pacific Rim" is at the front of the book? Why is "Looking Ahead" near the end?* In general, help students understand the logical arrangement of the contents page and how it can be used to quickly find main headings.

Indexes

- Turn to an index. Show students that the entries are arranged in alphabetical order. Explain the conventions of page numbering such as single pages separated by commas and multiple, consecutive pages indicated by a dash.
- Have students practice using the index to find specific information. For example, *Turn to any page that mentions Mexico. Show me the main section about New Zealand.*

Glossaries

- Have students skim a book's text and list all the words in the body, excluding headings, that are in boldfaced type. Then have them write those words in alphabetical order. Turn to the glossary and ask *What do you notice?* (The words and order should be the same.)
- Read through glossary entries with students. Then challenge students to suggest why these specific words have been chosen for inclusion. Ensure everyone understands that glossaries contain only words that are directly related to the book's subject.

Bibliographies

- Turn to page 31 of *Good Sports*. Show the students the "Bibliography" section, and together read the entries. Can students explain that a bibliography is a list of materials the author used to find information for writing the book?
- Highlight that the entries are in alphabetical order. Discuss the other conventions used: author's surname first; title in italicized type next; the name of the publisher; and finally, the year of publishing. Show students how to conduct a library search using these entries.

Headings

- Turn to any main section of a Student Book and read the heading to students. Ask *What information would you expect to find on this page?* Talk about how authors try to compose headings that clearly indicate what will be included in the body text.
- Turn to another main section and use a self-adhesive notepaper to cover the heading. Read the page to students and then have them brainstorm appropriate headings. Unmask the heading and discuss it in the context of the students' choices.

Subheadings

Turn to a page such as page 14 in *Water Wise* with the heading "Dirty Water." Show students how the author could have chosen to use subheadings (perhaps "Causes" and "Solutions" in this example) to present the information in another logical and clear way.

Labels

- Turn to a page featuring labels, such as page 4 in *Shake, Rumble, and Roll*. Point to the labels and show students that the accompanying body text often refers to these labels. Turn to another page, such as page 11 or 13 in the example book, and have students read the labels. Then have students search for text that refers to each label.
- Discuss how a label helps readers clarify their understandings of the related text.

Captions

Choose a page with captioned text. Discuss how the text in the caption(s) is about the image, and the two together present a more complete picture. For example, on pages 6 and 7 of *Frontiers of Technology*, have students read and discuss the relationship between the numbered captions and the diagram. Challenge them to think about why the author didn't use bullets. (Reasons might be there would be too much text or that this format presents a clearer picture.)

Bullets

Turn to a page containing bullets—page 7 of *Good Sports*, for example. Show students how using bullets is a way of highlighting and summarizing information. Then choose a suitable page without bullets, like page 8 of *Good Sports*, and help students rewrite the text in bulleted format.

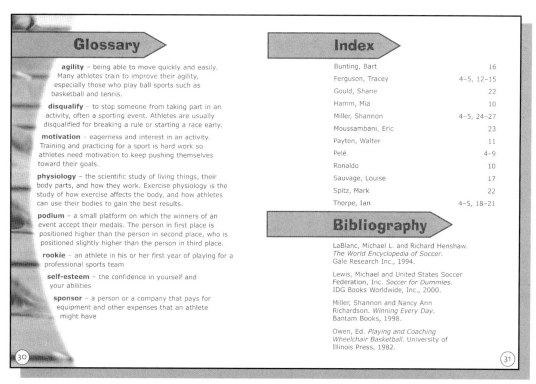

EXAMPLE OF THE GLOSSARY, INDEX, AND BIBLIOGRAPHY FROM *GOOD SPORTS*

Tips for Developing Visual Literacy

There are many visual elements throughout the series to reflect the many that students will need to use well in the world. The main focus of teaching to develop visual literacy is to help students use these elements so they can gain optimum meaning and ultimately be able to produce similar elements. Being visually literate, students can better demonstrate understanding, record information, and communicate.

Photographs and Illustrations

- Read a page heading to the students, and then cover the rest of the text. Have the students carefully study the illustration. Invite them to articulate all the information they gain from the illustration alone. Then uncover the text and have students read it. Ask *How did seeing the illustration help you read the text?*
- Have the students look at combinations of visual elements and text. For example, using pages 20–21 of *Shores of Freedom*, say *What are these people doing? What is important about the illustrations involving the musical instruments?* Discuss the students' responses and then read the text on these pages. Discuss how the combination of illustrations help in understanding the text.
- Turn to a page featuring a photograph. Discuss the differences in composition between photographs and illustrations. Help the students understand why an author would choose to use one instead of the other (detail required, photo opportunity, and so on).

Diagrams

- Ask about a diagram *How do we read it? Where do we start? Can we start in different places?* Write the text from the diagram on a chart, and read through it with students. Compare the chart with the diagram to lead into a discussion about how having both the text and diagram helps a reader achieve a better understanding.
- Lead students in comparing and contrasting a variety of diagrams. A few you might focus on are on page 21 of *Water Wise*, pages 6–7 of *The Green Scene*, page 25 of *Eye on the Ball*, and pages 20–21 of *Cell City*. Can students generalize that a diagram is a visual that is made to clearly show what something is, how it works, or the relation between parts?

Maps and Keys

- Discuss different kinds of keys—ones with letters, numbers, colors, symbols, and patterns. Then work with a map and accompanying key, such as on page 12 of *Spice It Up!* or page 4 in *Wild Planet*. Demonstrate and have students practice using the key to find a specific fact from the map. Help students understand that this can be an efficient and comprehensive way of presenting certain types of information.
- Students can compose their own maps of the school or neighborhood, complete with keys.

Cutaways

- Turn to a cutaway and carefully look at the illustration. Talk about how without cutaways, there would need to be two separate illustrations, and the effect would be lost.
- Turn to page 7 of *A Way with Words*. Ask students how the cutaway section helps them better understand how we are able to make sounds.

Cross Sections

- Locate a suitable cross section, for example, on pages 15–18 of *Shake, Rumble, and Roll*. Explain how this visual is similar to a cutaway but often much more expansive and designed to show an entire picture from both the outside and inside.
- Demonstrate how cross sections usually include text and sometimes include keys or arrows indicating movement.

Tables

- Have students recall examples of tables they are familiar with (weight, height, sports information, and so on). Talk about how tables are a useful way of displaying numerical information.
- Students can take a simple survey such as about eye and hair color and compose a table of results.

Charts

- Locate one or more charts in the Student Books. Help students understand that charts are used as a way of presenting text material, much the same way that tables are used to present numerical data.
- Read through a chart, making sure that students understand how a lot of information can be simply displayed in this format.

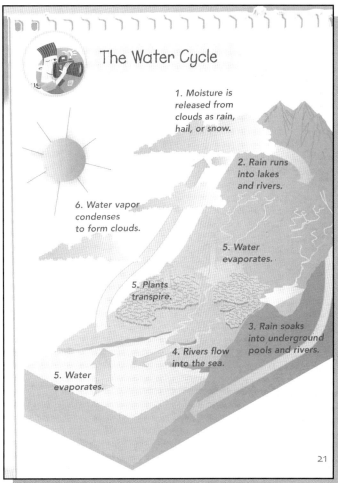

EXAMPLE OF A WATER CYCLE DIAGRAM FROM *WATER WISE*

Graphs

- Choose a page displaying a graph. Page 11 of *A Way with Words* has a bar graph, for example. Discuss the contrasting colors used to represent each language. Ask *Which is the most spoken language? How can you tell?* Then have students practice finding and interpreting information from the graph.
- Review other types of graphs the students may be familiar with, including line and pie graphs. Discuss when the use of these might be appropriate, and then have students compose bar, line, and pie graphs for a set of provided or gathered facts to see which graph best portrays the data.

Time Lines

- Select a time line. You might choose the one on pages 16–17 of *Ancient China*. Point out that the dates and events are arranged in chronological order. Help students understand that making a time line is a good way to visually display a rate of change or to memorialize important events.
- Students can compose time lines featuring important events in their lives.

Sparking Discussions and Research

Research Reading

To a large extent, the ultimate goal of any worthwhile literacy program is to have the students able to recognize their own needs and work independently in achieving their own goals. In the early stages of independence, it will be important to select appropriate research questions for individual students. It is equally important to model and review discovered examples of different ways the results of research can be communicated.

Each of the Student Book teaching notes, pp. 40–119, has a list of suggested research questions for independent readers, and the "Research Starters" in each Student Book is also a good source. The www.rigbyinfoquest.com information included in each Student Book's teaching notes also provides research questions that are answered on the Web site.

When your students become more independent with reporting and researching results in a variety of ways, you may want to have them set their own research questions and make their own decisions about how to display and report their findings.

Using the Research Starters

The "Research Starters" page at the end of each Student Book can be used in different ways, either before reading or after reading the book.

Choices Before Reading

- Choose one of the four research starters and invite groups of students to brainstorm what they already know. The group can next research further and report back. You can then combine all the groups' findings into a major list. This can either be added to as the book is read or amended after the book has been read.
- Assign a different research starter to pairs or small groups of students. After their research, have them report back to the large group. Then have the large group suggest other possible answers and useful sources for research.
- Choose a research starter; have students search the contents page and the index for page references they think will help them acquire information to answer the question.
- Choose a research starter for groups of students to research and present their findings in the form of a debate.

Choices After Reading

- The activities above will also be appropriate after the book has been read.
- Choose one research starter and have students review their reading of the text and visuals to gather information.
- Assign different research starters to small groups of students. Have the students list all the new information they gained to answer as a result of having read the text. Each research starter and list can then be shared with the rest of the class and expanded.
- Have students choose a research starter to research possible answers, perhaps as a homework activity.
- When students have explored one or more of the research starters, have them generate a list of further questions they can research.

Suggestions for Using the Web Site

Each Student Book contains a reference to Siteseeing on the www.rigbyinfoquest.com Web site. The site is a source of extra information about a specific topic and two learning activities for each book, all thematically connected to students' reading. Please see the Student Book Overview, pp. 36–39 of this resource, for a complete listing of the on-site topics.

When students have read a Student Book and go to its accompanying Web pages, they will find the first three pages have a question-and-answer format. There are up to six questions included. These questions are listed for your reference in the teaching notes for each book on pp. 40–119.

When appropriate, students can access the site as a homework activity. They can be assigned to research and complete one or both activities. Alternatively, individual or groups of students could be given questions to research within the classroom setting and then present the results in different ways. All the activities can be printed. If the students are working at home, you will need to ensure that they have their user name and that they know the address of the site.

You can assign and encourage students to present their understanding of information using a range of formats. Presentations may include written questions and answers, newspaper or magazine-style articles, interviews, visual or electronic displays, and oral presentations.

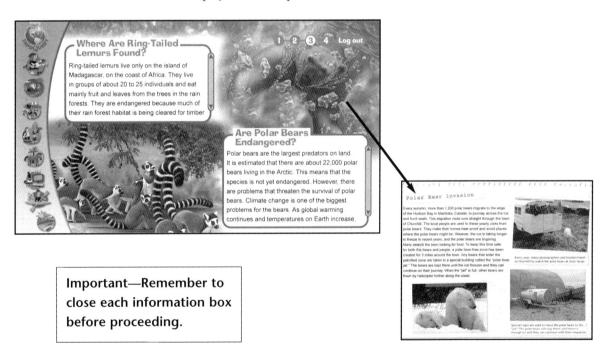

Important—Remember to close each information box before proceeding.

Extending with Special Content Features

Considering students' needs, valuable extensions of their learning, and your curriculum, you can make the most of the special content features in each Student Book of *Rigby InfoQuest*. Besides using Research Starters and the Web Siteseeing connection, these activities are suggested as general guidelines for the other features.

Word Builder

- Have students use a dictionary to generate more words from word parts.
- Use the target word to find more words with their origins in other languages.
- Begin to compose a glossary of new words.
- Begin a chart that includes new words, their origins, and other related words or synonyms and antonyms.
- When appropriate, use the words in Word Builder as a source of spelling words to learn or topics to write about.

Fast Facts

- Have students read the Fast Facts question on the "Features" page and respond to it before reading the Fast Facts.
- Begin a list of interesting Fast Facts, so the students can continue to add to it and use the list as a classroom source in later research or writing.
- Use the Fast Facts to help generate research questions.

Try This!

- Have students follow the instructions and complete the activity.
- Use the Try This! format to help students generate their own procedural text.
- Begin a class file (perhaps of hobbies, recipes, and so on) of written procedural text that the students can refer to for ideas.
- Set up a Try This! area in your classroom. Permission is given by the publisher to photocopy the Try This! activities for this purpose. Paste an activity onto a card, and put it with the required materials in the Try This! area. The students might even take the Try This! cards home for homework activities.

Techtalk

- Use the terms in Techtalk to begin a class glossary of technical terms.
- Generate research questions based on the information contained in Techtalk.
- Have students write about how a particular piece of technology affects them personally.

In Focus

- Because of text complexity, the In Focus features may best be approached by reading to or sharing the reading with students. As you explore these features together, discuss why the In Focus was included in a particular section and its relevance to the topic.
- Help students recognize the main point(s) of an In Focus. Then write and jumble the main points to have students place them in the correct sequence.
- Have students generate and investigate research questions from these features.
- Demonstrate and then have students rewrite an In Focus text in another form, such as bulleted or outline.

In the News
- Highlight the format of news articles, including headlines, dates and places, bylines, paragraphs, and photographs.
- Have students search local newspapers for related information.
- Use a topic of interest to begin a class newspaper.
- Use a particular news article to generate a range of research questions.

Profile
- Because of text complexity, the Profile features may best be read to the students or by sharing the reading. In discussion, you can help students understand biographical format such as chronology, key dates, main points, and so on.
- Use the Profile feature to generate research questions.
- Have students use the format of Profile to write their own personal biographical sketches.
- Begin and add to a file of interesting people from the past. This could be arranged in chronological order.

Time Link
- Use the text of Time Link to demonstrate writing a time line.
- When appropriate, have students use an atlas, globe, or map to find the highlighted area.
- Use the Time Link feature to generate questions for students' research.
- Begin and add to a file of interesting facts from the past.

What's Your Opinion?
- Have students read the "for" and "against" arguments and justify responses.
- Groups of students could be encouraged to debate the issues.
- Have students write supporting statements for a position.

My Diary
- Use My Diary to demonstrate chronological writing.
- Use the information to generate research questions.
- Rewrite My Diary information in the form of a report.

Fact Finder
- Use the Fact Finder to generate research questions.
- Have students compose their own Fact Finder questions.

Earth Watch
- Have students form and justify opinions on specific issues.
- Students can research environmental issues that most interest them or apply to your area.
- Begin and add to a file of environmental issues.

EXAMPLE OF SPECIAL CONTENT FEATURES FROM *MATTER SPLATTER!*

Assessing and Evaluating

The belief that well-constructed learning activities are opportunities for authentic assessment is the guiding principle for assessment and evaluation throughout these resources. Activities for authentic assessment in *Rigby InfoQuest*

- are themselves valuable learning activities.
- occur throughout and after the reading of a text, and are a natural consequence of what has been read.
- provide immediate and ongoing feedback about learning to students and teachers.

Assessment concentrates on the students' abilities to understand and use the text and literary elements of nonfiction material. There are many opportunities for assessing the understanding and use of these highly important skills:

- recognizing important information
- forming generalizations
- evaluating facts and opinions
- comparing and contrasting
- sequencing and summarizing
- classifying and categorizing
- interpreting visual elements
- using text organizers

Provided Assessment Activities

For each Student Book, assessment tools for use during and after reading are provided in the Student Book Notes of this resource, pp. 40–119.

During Reading

The "Guiding Learning" section of each book's notes highlights key text and visual elements to discuss. Each of the activities can be assessed informally as the reading progresses, and the results will be a quick indicator of students' learning.

After Reading

Thinking Activity—For students' practice as well as assessment following each Student Book, a Thinking Activity blackline master involves the use of a key skill or skills. The completed worksheets will provide an ongoing record of students' progress in the main aspects of learning associated with nonfiction text.

Formal Assessment—Each Student Book's Nonfiction Assessment Record is a blackline master for taking more formal assessment. The Assessment Record is derived from the learning outcomes, purposes for reading, and critical thinking skills that can be your teaching focuses for the book. You may use all the sections to comprehensively assess student learning, or you may be selective and choose to assess fewer skills if that is appropriate for an individual student.

Optional Assessment and Evaluation Activities

As well as assessing students' abilities to understand and use the elements of nonfiction material, you may also wish to assess the way students use semantic, syntactic, and graphophonic information as they read. Cloze procedures can be used to find out the reading process skills and strategies that students are using.

Cloze procedures can be used with individual students whenever you feel the need for further assessment. You can either use self-adhesive strips on the selected text in a Student Book or photocopy short sections of text and blacken out the appropriate words.

Delete some function words (pronouns, conjunctions, prepositions, and adjectives) to check students' use of syntactic information.

→

Some changes take a _____ long time. Over millions _____ years, matter from plants _____ animals decays and is pressed together. This matter eventually changes _____ coal or oil. _____ changes, however, are sudden.

Delete some content words (nouns and verbs) to check students' use of semantic information.

→

Some changes take a very long _____. Over millions of _____, matter from plants and animals decays and is _____ together. This _____ eventually changes into coal or oil. Some changes, however, _____ sudden.

An Example of Planning and Use

The following is the extended lesson planning of one teacher. She has used the Student Book Notes provided for *Matter Splatter!*, considered the needs of a group of her students, and clarified her lesson goals by using the previously suggested 6-step planning for success model. This plan could be adapted and used with any of the titles in *Rigby InfoQuest*. The bolded sections are items that appear on the assessment master provided in the Notes for the book and show how the teacher plans to incorporate them into the group reading session before later individual assessment. The teacher has added explanations for some of her thinking.

1. Learning Outcomes

I want my students to successfully:
- be able to specify the three main states of matter.
- recall and describe what a solution is.
- display an understanding of how matter changes.

2. Purposes for Reading

The students need to know that the purposes for them reading the text are:
- to learn what matter is.
- to learn about some of the different types of matter.
- to learn how new types of matter are being created.
- to form and justify opinions about the use of plastics.

[Note: Appropriate purposes for the particular students have been chosen from both the "Purposes for Reading" and "Critical Thinking" possibilities listed in the Student Book Notes.]

3. Guiding the Reading

[This plan for reading the book may be spread out over several sessions, depending on our time available. I will use a mixture of approaches during the reading.]

Before Reading

- Assign pairs of students Research Starter Number 3 on page 32 of *Matter Splatter!* Provide time following their discussions for sharing their ideas with the group.
- Give the students time to look through *Matter Splatter!* Invite one student to find the contents page. Discuss its function. Locate the index and glossary, and discuss the functions they have. Read the words from the index and glossary to the students, and explain that these are words they'll be meeting in the text and learning to use.
- Tell students this book is all about matter. Ask, *What is matter? Are there different kinds? How are they different?* Begin a chart with the headings "Solids," "Liquids," and "Gases." Invite students to offer suggestions for what could be included under each heading. Record these. Continue adding to and amending the chart during the reading.

During Reading

[I'll remember to use vocabulary that is in the text as much as possible when asking questions to guide students' learning.]

- Pages 4–7: Discuss the illustrations and photographs on pages 4 and 5. I can say:
  – *Read page 4. Remember to use the glossary for bolded words. Find out what mass means.*

- Discuss the nature of matter. Invite students to find out more about matter.
  – *Read to the end of page 6 and find out how the three states of matter are different.*
  When the students have finished, **discuss the ways molecules are joined together in different states of matter**. Read page 7 to students. Ask, *Why was Rutherford's discovery important? How has it changed our lives today?*

- Pages 8–13: Have students read each double-page spread. Say, *Read to the end of page 13. As you are reading, make a written note of at least one thing that distinguishes each state of matter from the others.* If students need more support, share read sections of the text. **Then discuss the differences in the three states of matter**. (Solids keep their shapes; liquids take the shape of their containers; gases don't keep their shapes.)

- Pages 14–17: Ask, *What causes matter to change?* Have students use examples to discuss and justify their responses. Invite them to use the glossary to find the meaning of *decomposes*. Then have students read pages 14 and 15. **Discuss the importance of heat and friction in changing matter**. Ask, *Are all changes in matter permanent?* Challenge students to form and justify opinions about this before reading pages 16 and 17. Discuss permanence and the speed of change. Reread the diagram at the bottom of pages 16 and 17. Have students summarize this information.

- Pages 18–21: Read page 18 aloud. **Discuss and highlight the fact that solutions are created when solids are dissolved in liquids**. Help students to read and understand the diagram on page 19. Then ask, *Do you know what an alloy is?* Share read pages 20 and 21. Discuss some of the important contributions alloys make to our daily lives. Ask, *How would your life be different without alloys?* Have students discuss their responses.

- Pages 22–27: Say, *The next six pages deal with three special types of matter: plastics, cardboard, and adhesives, or glues. Read to the end of page 27 and write notes of at least two advantages of each of these materials.* Share read sections of the text with any students who require further support. When students have finished, have them share and compare what they have written. **Discuss some of the ways new materials are created. Then have students form and justify opinions about the use of plastics**. Say, *Do you think the benefits of plastics outweigh the dangers to the environment? Why/Why not?* Complete this section by having students discuss their ideas of any other practical or fantastic uses not mentioned in the text for these three types of materials.

- Pages 28–29: Tell students that the text on pages 28 and 29 is referred to as procedural text. Help students understand that procedural text involves explaining, step-by-step, how to do something. Talk about how the procedural text on these pages resembles a recipe. Share read to the end of page 29 and then discuss the steps. If possible, arrange to have the materials available for students' experimentation.

4. Modeling Responses

- Tell the students that they are going to be locating and recording important information from the book about matter. [Thinking Activity Master 11 will be used.]
- Demonstrate how to use the contents page, glossary, and index to locate specific information. Then discuss the activity sheet, ensuring students are clear about the requirements.

5. Responding and Extending

- Distribute individual copies of the activity worksheet and have students complete the exercise.
- When students have finished, we'll discuss the process involved. Have students compare and discuss their responses. Discuss the reasons some of the students' responses may have differed.

  Talk about how this type of approach could be used to summarize information from other nonfiction books.

[The following activities are my options for broadening and strengthening the learning outcomes and purposes for reading.]

Using the Index

Turn to the index. Remind that entries are in alphabetical order. Review the conventions of page numbering such as single pages separated by commas and multiple, consecutive pages indicated by a dash. Have students practice using the index to find specific facts.

Using the Features Page

Look at the headings and read these together. Have the students find the answers by turning to the relevant pages. They could work individually or in pairs.

Using the Web Site

- Pose questions to the students. [These are listed in the Student Book Notes.]
  1. What is physics?
  2. How are matter and energy connected?
  3. From where does energy come?
  4. What are some ways people use energy?
  5. What is potential energy?
  6. What is kinetic energy?

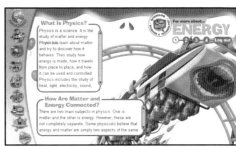

- Make a list of the students' ideas. Explain that the answers to these questions can be found on the Siteseeing Web site. If necessary, demonstrate how to access the site, the zone (Science & Technology) and the link (Energy).
- Provide time for the students to research these ideas independently or in pairs and then complete the activities. This may be done at school or at home.

6. Assessment

- Make copies of the Nonfiction Assessment Record (page 83) to use individually with each student. [The activities on the assessment sheet are directly linked to the learning outcomes, purposes for reading, and critical thinking skills for *Matter Splatter!* I will choose to either use the entire assessment sheet or highlight the specific areas I wish to assess for each student.]

- Depending on my observations during the reading and this assessment, I may also use cloze procedures and running records to assess some students' reading process skills.

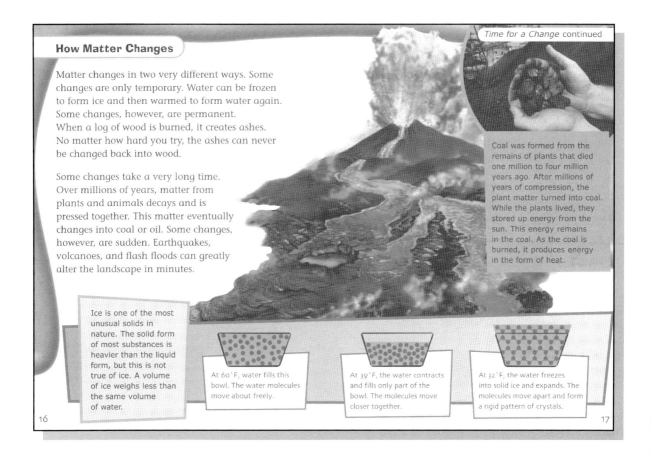

Time for a Change continued

How Matter Changes

Matter changes in two very different ways. Some changes are only temporary. Water can be frozen to form ice and then warmed to form water again. Some changes, however, are permanent. When a log of wood is burned, it creates ashes. No matter how hard you try, the ashes can never be changed back into wood.

Some changes take a very long time. Over millions of years, matter from plants and animals decays and is pressed together. This matter eventually changes into coal or oil. Some changes, however, are sudden. Earthquakes, volcanoes, and flash floods can greatly alter the landscape in minutes.

Coal was formed from the remains of plants that died one million to four million years ago. After millions of years of compression, the plant matter turned into coal. While the plants lived, they stored up energy from the sun. This energy remains in the coal. As the coal is burned, it produces energy in the form of heat.

Ice is one of the most unusual solids in nature. The solid form of most substances is heavier than the liquid form, but this is not true of ice. A volume of ice weighs less than the same volume of water.

At 60°F, water fills this bowl. The water molecules move about freely.

At 39°F, the water contracts and fills only part of the bowl. The molecules move closer together.

At 32°F, the water freezes into solid ice and expands. The molecules move apart and form a rigid pattern of crystals.

16

17

InfoMagazine Notes—*Art for Life*

Synopsis

Art for Life highlights the importance of art in making our world a more vibrant place. It explores the development of art from the earliest cave paintings to modern and digital art. Some enjoyable art activities for students are included.

Possible Teaching Points

The following teaching points can be selected for introductions or revisits to nonfiction text, skills, and organizers.
1. Recognizing Different Types of Text
2. Reading a Time Line
3. Forming Generalizations
4. Reading a Report
5. Forming and Justifying Opinions
6. Reading Procedural Text

Each of these teaching points can be assessed informally during the reading.

Visual Elements

Opportunities exist throughout the text to explore the following visual elements.
- a variety of illustrations and photographs
- sections divided by design elements
- a captioned time line
- illustrated procedural text

Special Features

Opportunities exist to introduce or extend cross-curricular learning.
- "Time Link" presents a time line of important art and artists.
- "Try This!" features art activities to try.
- "In Focus" explores the styles in art by five artists.
- "What's Your Opinion?" lets you have your say about environmental art.

Reading the InfoMagazine

Before Reading

Read the title to students and ask, *Why is art important to people? Where are some places art can be found?* Have students discuss these questions and then begin a web showing different places art can be found. Add to this as the reading of the text progresses.

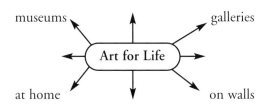

Sharing the Text

Although the following suggestions involve your reading aloud and shared reading, more capable students can be given guide questions and read independently. (See pages 12–13.)

Recognizing Different Types of Text

Pages 2–5: Have students look carefully at pages 2 and 3 and predict which sections they'll find most interesting. Read pages 4 and 5 to students. Talk about the functions of art in the past. Then have students reread all the text on page 4 to discuss some of the differences between the expository and report formats.

Informal Assessment: Have students rewrite the introductory paragraph on page 4 in past tense and in the form of a report.

Reading a Time Line

Pages 6–7: Share read these pages. Discuss the different types of art highlighted and help students see some of the style differences as well as how art has progressed.

Informal Assessment: Challenge students to state why the time line in the beginning spans many years but later spans smaller periods of time.

Forming Generalizations

Pages 8–11: Share read these pages and talk about the importance of portraits in earlier times and how art has changed over the last few centuries.

Informal Assessment: Have students reread pages 10 and 11 before offering a generalization about the main difference between traditional and abstract art.

Reading a Report

Pages 12–15: Share read these pages. Help students talk about the variety of static and mobile art forms. Have students reread the report on Francis Salole on page 15. Discuss some of the similarities between the report form and a newspaper article.

Informal Assessment: Have students search for and rewrite important information from the report on Francis Salole in bulleted point form.

Forming and Justifying Opinions

Pages 18–21: Share read these pages. Have students discuss the reasons people are interested in environmental art. Then have students reread and discuss the section about Christo.

Informal Assessment: Challenge students to form and justify an opinion about whether or not Christo and Jeanne-Claude's bridge was art.

Reading Procedural Text

Pages 22–23: Read through these pages with students. Discuss the match between the illustrations and the step-by-step instructions. Challenge students to state how this procedural text is similar to a recipe format.

Informal Assessment: Have students use the procedural text to complete one or more of the activities.

After Reading

Complete the *Art for Life* web from the "Before Reading" session.

InfoMagazine Master A
Did You Know? Summarizing Important Information

Talk about how authors sometimes write important information in the form of "Did You Know?" answers. Discuss how these are usually written using concise language and including the most important or interesting facts about a topic. Then read through the instructions and example on the activity sheet.

InfoMagazine Master B
Different Types of Art: Locating and Matching Information

Discuss using the contents pages to find information. Then read through the activity instructions with students.

Did You Know?

Name _____   Date _____

Use the contents pages in *Art for Life* to find information. Then reread and write an exciting "Did You Know?" fact for each of the topics below.

Digital Art
_____

_____

_____

_____

Abstract Art
_____

_____

_____

_____

Art for Life—Did You Know?

Environmental Art
_____

_____

_____

Cave Art
_____

_____

_____

Art That Moves
_____

_____

_____

_____

Different Types of Art

Name _____ Date _____

Draw a line to match each type of art with its description.

Type of Art	Description
Impressionism	uses only colors and shapes
self-portraits	uses popular culture as the subject
mosaic	art involving moving parts
pop	art out in the open
prehistoric	from the "rebirth" period
abstract	made with chips of material
environmental	pictures that artists make of themselves
batik	dabs of pure color mixed on canvas
kinetic	art found in ancient caves
Renaissance	involves using hot wax and dye

InfoMagazine Notes—*Spotlight on Spiders*

Synopsis

Spotlight on Spiders presents a comprehensive look at the fascinating lives of spiders. It includes detailed information about the differences between spiders and insects, different kinds of spiders, and their attack and defense strategies.

Possible Teaching Points

The following teaching points can be selected for introductions or revisits to nonfiction text, skills, and organizers.
1. Using the Contents Pages
2. Reading Diagrams with Labels
3. Interpreting a Flow Diagram
4. Comparing and Contrasting Information
5. Summarizing Text Information
6. Forming and Justifying Opinions

Each of these teaching points can be assessed informally during the reading.

Visual Elements

Opportunities exist throughout the text to explore the following visual elements.
- diagrams with leadered labels
- captioned illustrations and photographs
- cartoon-style illustrations
- a flow diagram
- a Venn diagram

Special Features

Opportunities exist to introduce or extend cross-curricular learning.
- "In Focus" features the role of a spider inspector.
- "Word Builder" explains the connection between spiders and ancient Greek mythology.
- "Profile" highlights the role of a "bug man" in making movies.
- "Fast Facts" presents what tarantulas have in common with a dance.

Reading the InfoMagazine

Before Reading

Read the title to students and ask, *Are spiders insects? How do you know? Why are some people afraid of spiders?* Have students discuss these questions and then begin a KWL chart. Continue to work together on this chart as the reading of the text continues. For example:

What We Think We **Know** About Spiders	Were We Right?	What We **Want** to Know About Spiders	What We **Learned** About Spiders
Spiders have eight legs.	yes	How are spiders and insects different?	
Some spiders are dangerous.			

Sharing the Text

Although the following suggestions involve your reading aloud and shared reading, more capable students can be given guide questions and read independently. (See pages 12–13.)

Using the Contents Pages

Pages 2–3: Have students look carefully at this spread and discuss how this compares to other contents pages. Have students say what information they expect to find in each section, and then select individuals to turn to the appropriate sections and check their assumptions. Stress the fact that any contents pages help the reader locate broad topics.

Informal Assessment: Have students use the contents pages. Ask questions such as, *On which page would we find information about a spider's sight?*

Reading Diagrams with Labels

Pages 4–7: Share read the body text on these pages. Return to pages 4 and 5. Discuss the placement of labels and how the body text relates to the diagram. Ask, *How does the illustration help you better understand the parts of the spiders?*

Informal Assessment: Have students refer to the diagrams. Ask, *What are the two main body parts? Where are the eyes?*

Interpreting a Flow Diagram

Pages 8–9: Share read these pages and talk about the text layout. Discuss the content and why the author may have chosen to use a flow diagram. Challenge students to suggest other ways this information could have been presented.

Informal Assessment: Challenge students to reread the flow diagram and write a different heading for each section.

Comparing and Contrasting Information

Pages 10–13: Share read these pages. Discuss why the author decided to separate these types of spiders. Highlight how the author has presented general information in the body text of each spread and followed it with detailed examples.

Informal Assessment: Have students reread these pages and find as many similarities and differences between the magazine's "Web Page" and "Hairy Hunters" sections as they can.

Summarizing Text Information

Pages 14–17: Share read these pages. Challenge students to summarize the main points presented about tarantulas. Then demonstrate how these could be written in bulleted form.

Informal Assessment: Have students reread "Spider Defense" and then summarize this section in bulleted form.

Forming and Justifying Opinions

Pages 18–21: Either share read or read these pages to students. Help students understand the different reactions to spiders that people have. Ask, *How have literature and movies helped shape people's opinions about spiders?*

Informal Assessment: Encourage students to form and justify an opinion about spiders. Ask, *Should people be afraid of spiders? Why/Why not?*

After Reading

Allow some time for students to complete the activities on pages 22 and 23. Then complete the KWL chart from the "Before Reading" session.

InfoMagazine Master C
Spider Fact Web: Locating and Recording Information

Demonstrate using the contents pages and page headings to locate information. Discuss the difference between important and secondary information. Then have students complete the activity.

InfoMagazine Master D
A Spider Diary: Summarizing Information

Emphasize the diary format (chronology, informal language, etc.). Then have students choose one type of spider from the book and write about a possible observed day in the life of that spider.

Student Books—Overview

Title	Key Content	Learning Outcomes	Critical Thinking	Visual Elements	
A Way with Words	how language began the vocal chords fun with languages accents/dialects	why communication is essential to humans how language varies importance of the printing press	sequencing language development forming/justifying opinions creating a word puzzle	sequential diagrams diagrams with labels diagrams with captioned text double-page spreads	
Ancient China	life in ancient China China's contributions to the modern world Chinese dynasties	how China developed ancient Chinese defenses Chinese advances in writing	generalizing about family life forming opinions summarizing information	map with labels leaders to captions gatefold pages double-page spreads procedural diagram	
Cell City	human body cells keeping ourselves healthy the major body organs	functions of cells understanding the nervous system how lungs work	summarizing brain functions forming generalizations completing a chart	cross-sectional diagrams cutaway diagram double-page spreads	
Dynamic Dance	historical dance origins types of dance availability of dance to all people	importance of dance main tasks of a choreographer the universal nature of folk dance	sequencing the development of ballet comparing performance and social dance summarizing key facts	illustrated diary entries double-page spreads illustrations and photographs	
Eye on the Ball	historical origins of ball sports sports development variety of modern ball sports	amateur and professional differences in sports technology in sports features of specific sports	comparing/contrasting ball sports justifying opinions inventing a new ball game	diagram with arrows to text gatefold pages illustrations and photographs	
Frontiers of Technology	how technology changes lives advances in travel advances in medical science	how computers have changed education protecting resources how robots can be useful to people	generalizing 20th century predictions justifying opinions making predictions about technology	cutaway diagrams captioned illustrations double-page spreads illustrations and photographs	
Getting Together	types of clubs and groups why people form friendships effects of conforming	why people group together advantages of Scouts and Guides how people become citizens	justifying opinions about school uniforms forming generalizations about fashion summarizing information for a new club	cartoon-style illustrations thought bubbles double-page spreads illustrations and photographs	
Good Sports	qualities of athletes paraplegic athletes function and format of bibliographies	why Pelé is the world's best soccer player Shannon Millar's accomplishments how to improve in a sport	summarizing information sequencing time line information creating a profile of an athlete	map with a key time line illustrations and photographs double-page spreads	
It's Show Time	different uses of stilts roles of street performers performance training	traditional stilt usage importance of non-traditional circuses skills required to be a clown	generalizing why people perform forming opinions about animals in circuses summarizing in a diary	map with captions photographs and illustrations double-page spreads	
Lands of Rock	features of canyons recreational opportunities underground environments	why rocks change shape why fossils are important different uses of rocky environments	generalizing about rock dwellings interpreting maps composing a map with a key and symbols	maps with a symbol key captioned text symbol-supported text photographs and illustrations	

Vocabulary Development	Text Types	Comprehension Skill Activity Master	Assessment	Siteseeing www.rigby infoquest.com
accent, dialect, hieroglyphic, instinctive, larynx, oral, scribe, sibling, slang, trachea, volume	time line labeled graph biography persuasive text	Thinking Activity Master 1: using the index and glossary to create a puzzle	function of the larynx interpreting a time line how technology is changing written language	Zone: Art & Entertainment Link: Language
acupuncture, ancestor, artisan, calligraphy, class, dynasty, embroider, generation, Silk Road, terra-cotta	procedural text time line expository text historical excerpt	Thinking Activity Master 2: summarizing information and using heightened language	how China developed family life in China contributions of Chinese to modern society	Zone: People & Places Link: Ancient China
bacteria, carbohydrate, enzyme, intestine, melanin, mineral, nutrient, organ, pigment, tissue, vertebrae, vitamin	diary format inset safety tips procedural text expository text	Thinking Activity Master 3: locating and recording information in the form of a chart	main functions of cells and the nervous system how lungs work different kinds of cells	Zone: Science & Technology Link: Health Science
apartheid, banquet, choreographer, indigenous, Renaissance period, Romantic period	historical text biography interview expository text	Thinking Activity Master 4: locating and summarizing key facts in the text	key benefits of dance main changes to ballet over the years different types of dance	Zone: Art & Entertainment Link: Dance
archaeology, historian, media, official, publicity, sponsor, synthetic	historical text newspaper report expository text biography	Thinking Activity Master 5: using text information to invent a new ball sport	using text organizers development of a range of sports how technology has changed sports	Zone: Sports & Adventure Link: Ball Games
acceleration force, amputee, genetically engineered, infectious, intranet, levitate, microchip, molecule, mutation, prosthetic, virtual reality	interview biography historical perspective expository text	Thinking Activity Master 6: making predictions about technological advances in the future	benefits of inventions in the home importance of prosthetics how robots can help in the future	Zone: Science & Technology Link: Transportation Technology
ballot, conform, democracy, extended family, motto, naturalization, nuclear family, peer pressure, society, social science	bullet points historical perspective expository text	Thinking Activity Master 7: summarizing information in order to imagine a new type of club	why people group together what dictates fashion advantages of Scouts and Guides becoming a citizen	Zone: People & Places Link: Identity
agility, disqualify, motivation, physiology, podium, rookie, self-esteem, sponsor	newspaper reports biographies diary format expository text	Thinking Activity Master 8: composing, sequencing, and summarizing information in the form of a profile	summarizing athletes' qualities reasons for inclusion of bibliographies overcoming a handicap	Zone: Sports & Adventure Link: Sports
acrobatics, cast, comedian, improvise, minstrel, prop, puppeteer, slapstick, tip, troupe	interview diary format profile expository text	Thinking Activity Master 9: summarizing information in the form of a diary	different roles of street performers importance of alternative circuses skills required to perform	Zone: Art & Entertainment Link: Puppets
alpine, ascend, badlands, bouldering, canyon, crevasse, descend, geologist, mesa, monolith, paleontologist, pictograph, plateau, summit	diary format profiles expository text cartoon-supported text	Thinking Activity Master 10: composing a map with a key and symbols	reasons why rocks change shape why the study of fossils is important opportunities for recreation in rock lands	Zone: Sports & Adventure Link: Mountain Climbing

nt Books—Overview

e	Key Content	Learning Outcomes	Critical Thinking	Visual Elements	
Matter Splatter!	the nature of matter different types of matter creating new types of matter	three main states of matter description of a solution how matter changes	comparing ways that matter changes justifying opinions locating and recording important information	sequenced diagrams process directions with illustrations diagrams and photographs	
People of the Pacific Rim	settlement of the Pacific Rim the variety of people foods of the Pacific Rim	why Rim volcanoes and earthquakes occur why there is increased population movement why tales were told	generalizing about economies interpreting a trade route map writing a recipe	maps with keys double-page spreads time lines captioned photographs and illustrations	
Shake, Rumble, and Roll	main effects of earthquakes disaster safety major natural disasters	what causes volcanoes and earthquakes dangers associated with volcanoes what tsunamis are	generalizing about eruptions interpreting a map writing a newspaper article	cross-sectional diagram sequenced captioned diagrams Richter scale	
Shores of Freedom	why people emigrated life in the 13 colonies events before the American Revolution	why Pilgrims left Europe the Acadian movement to Louisiana the significance of Magellan's voyage	comparing colonial and present times summarizing European life during the 1600s completing a time line	maps with labels map with captioned text double-page spreads	
Spice It Up!	different spices spices and exploration changing value of spices	difference between herbs and spices importance of salt importance of spices in ancient times	summarizing chili pepper information justifying opinions about spice trade using information in a pie graph	maps with arrows and keys illustrations with labels double-page spreads	
The Green Scene	nature of ecosystems interaction in a food chain protecting our biosphere	tasks of ecologists Earth's biomes symbiotic relationships	summarizing differences interpreting a diagram of a food chain researching, gathering, and organizing facts	labeled diagrams double-page spreads comparison chart food chain diagrams	
The Test of Time	development of inventions famous inventors how some inventions were named	why inventions stood the test of time technology leading to invention inventions from different time periods	justifying opinions about inventions sequencing information about development composing interview questions	illustrated time lines captioned illustrations double-page spreads historical photographs	
Water Wise	different forms of water the water cycle the problem of global warming	importance of water changing state causes of water pollution home water supplies	interpreting a rainfall map justifying opinions organizing information and using headings	pie graph map with a key sequenced diagrams numbered illustrations with a key	
What a Century!	life in different 20th century decades unrest in the 1960s and 1970s famous discoveries	reasons for change how life has changed throughout decades 21st century challenges	comparing postwar life justifying opinions about events matching information and dates	historical photographs information in game format illustrations with captioned text	
Wild Planet	importance of ecosystems species adaptation endangered animals	why species become endangered introduced species helping endangered animals	justifying opinions forming generalizations about food chains summarizing facts in chart form	maps with captions text with bullet points diary format photographs and illustrations	

Vocabulary Development	Text Types	Comprehension Skill Activity Master	Assessment	Siteseeing www.rigby infoquest.com
atom, compress, decompose, evaporate, expand, flammable, invisible, mass, molecule, polymer, resin, viscous	biography procedural text interview expository text	Thinking Activity Master 11: locating and recording important information in the form of a web	different states of matter what a solution is creation of plastics or polymers	Zone: Science & Technology Link: Energy
anthropologist, balsa, emigrate, export, import, indigenous, luxury goods, Pacific plate, primary products, tamales, tourism	newspaper report procedural text time line expository text interview	Thinking Activity Master 12: using text organizers and symbols to write a recipe	reasons for exploration importance of seafood to the region understanding natural resources	Zone: People & Places Link: Pacific Pastimes
convection currents, dormant, evacuate, fault, friction, magma, magnitude, Richter scale, state of emergency, subduction, tremor	historical text newspaper report expository text instructional text	Thinking Activity Master 13: locating and summarizing information in the form of a newspaper article	main causes of volcanoes and earthquakes dangers associated with volcanoes minimizing risk	Zone: Past & Future Link: Pompeii
convict, descendant, independence, military, patriotic, penal colony, Pilgrim, plague, Puritan, replica, treaty	historical text biographies expository text poetry	Thinking Activity Master 14: locating important information in order to complete a time line	why people chose to live in different lands events leading to the Revolutionary War colonial life	Zone: Past & Future Link: Early Colonies
aroma, bland, circumnavigation, cuisine, condiment, cultivate, currency, Far East, garnish, incense, monopoly, orchid, season, stigma, temperate	historical text procedural text tongue twister expository text	Thinking Activity Master 15: gathering and using information in the form of a pie graph	how spices changed world exploration different ways chilies are used the importance of salt in our diets	Zone: People & Places Link: Spices
biodegradable, biodiversity, conserve, mutual, organism, variable	procedural text newspaper report expository text bulleted points	Thinking Activity Master 16: researching, gathering, and organizing facts about biomes	tasks of ecologists what constitutes an ecosystem importance of symbiosis helping our own biosphere	Zone: Plants & Animals Link: Ecology
Industrial Revolution, invention, laser, mass production, millennia, patent, phonograph, prototype, Renaissance, zeppelin	biographical text historical text expository text	Thinking Activity Master 17: recognizing and recording important information in the form of an interview	reading a time line how inventors name their inventions why some inventions didn't stand the test of time	Zone: Science & Technology Link: Space Technology
dehydrate, evaporation, reservoir, sanitation, transportation, watershed	poetry instructional text historical text expository text	Thinking Activity Master 18: gathering and organizing information by using headings	reading a rainfall map understanding water pollution parts of the water cycle water conservation	Zone: Water, Earth, & Sky Link: Water
alliance, civil rights, communist, democratic, dictatorship, New Deal, oil crisis, stock market, United Nations	historical text expository text diary newspaper report biography	Thinking Activity Master 19: locating and matching information and dates in the 20th century	why people are now generally better off reasons for protest 21st century challenges 20th century inventions	Zone: Art & Entertainment Link: Entertainment
adapt, alien, Earth summit, ecosystem, endangered, exotic, habitat, poach, refuge	diary report expository text	Thinking Activity Master 20: summarizing information in the form of a KWL chart	maintaining ecosystems the problem of introduced species how to help endangered species	Zone: Plants & Animals Link: Endangered Animals

Student Book Notes—*A Way with Words*

Synopsis

A Way with Words highlights the importance of language as part of human culture. The book explores the growth of both oral and written language and how these have developed differences throughout the world.

Vocabulary Development
accent, dialect, hieroglyphic, instinctive, larynx, oral, scribe, sibling, slang, trachea, volume

Challenges in the Text
time line; graph

Cross-Curricular Connections
language arts; social studies; technology

Learning Outcomes

Students will:

1. be able to state why communication is essential to humans.
2. state why the development of the printing press was very important.
3. understand how the same language varies in different regions.

For Independent Readers

Provide these questions before students read the text:

- How are human and animal communications similar and different?
- How do children learn to talk?
- Which languages are most widely spoken throughout the world?
- How has language changed?

Visual Elements

Students have the opportunity to:

1. view sequential diagrams.
2. read diagrams with labels.
3. read diagrams with captioned text.
4. view double-page spreads.

Purposes for Reading

Possible choices include:

1. to learn about the way speech sounds are produced.
2. to learn about how language has changed in the past and is still changing.
3. to learn how technology has influenced language.

Critical Thinking

Students have the opportunity to:

1. sequence language development in chronological order.
2. form and justify opinions about the need for a universal language.
3. use the index and glossary to compose a crossword or word find puzzle.

Special Features

- Should everyone speak the same language? Read "What's Your Opinion?" and decide.
- Check out "Profile" to discover who wrote a play about accents.
- Decode text messages with "Fact Finder."

Guiding Learning

Before Reading

Discuss some colloquial language that students use. Take an example like "*awesome.*" Ask, *What would your parents have said?* Make a list of responses (*cool, groovy,* etc.) Then have students discuss why they think language changes.

During Reading

Key text to guide:

Pages 4–5: Read aloud and then highlight differences between animal and human communications. Point out the English word *Hello,* and have students find and comment on the other greetings as the reading progresses. (*The greetings are: p. 7 Thai; p. 9 Spanish; p. 11 Maori; p. 13 Esperanto; p. 15 Kiswahili (Swahili); p. 16 French; p. 19 Afrikaans; p. 20 Mandarin; p. 22 Italian; p. 25 Hebrew; p. 29 Hindi*)

Pages 6–7: Share read. Help students understand the diagram and the roles of the larynx, vocal cords, and trachea.

Pages 8–9: Have students read the body text before share reading the time line. Ask probing questions to establish students' understanding of the order of development.

Pages 10–15: Have students read independently. When finished, discuss the graph on page 11. Then ask, *Do you think there should be only one world language?* Challenge students to justify their opinions.

Pages 16–23: Say, *Language is always changing. Read to the end of page 23 to find out how and why language has changed.* (Share read with students needing support.) When students have finished, discuss what they have found out. Help them understand the diagram on page 19 and why the invention of the printing press was highly important. Then have students interpret the text messages on page 23.

Pages 24–27: Say, *How was your name chosen? Who chose it?* After students have responded, have them read independently. Discuss the different ways children are named throughout the world.

Pages 28–29: Read these pages aloud as there is fun solving the riddles. Allow time for student pairs to write word staircases.

After Reading

Responding: Have students discuss what they have learned about language changes. Ask, *How might language change in the future?* Have them justify their responses.

Thinking Activity Master 1

A Puzzler: Using an Index and a Glossary

Demonstrate beginning a word find and a crossword puzzle by using the index or glossary. Discuss conventions involved, including "across and down" clues. Then students can compose a crossword puzzle or a simpler word find puzzle by using the book. Students can trade to complete a puzzler.

www.rigbyinfoquest.com

Zone: Art & Entertainment
Link: Language

Students can research answers on the site:

1. When did crossword puzzles begin?
2. What is an anagram?
3. What is a palindrome?
4. What are malapropisms?
5. Why did people begin using surnames?

Learning Activities

Students can complete activities on the site:

- Search the neighborhood for surnames based on occupations.
- Use a dictionary to search for word origins.

SITESEEING • ART & ENTERTAINMENT •
When did crossword puzzles begin?
Visit www.rigbyinfoquest.com
for more about LANGUAGE.

A Puzzler

Name _____   Date _____

Use the index and glossary in *A Way with Words* to find information and create a crossword or word find puzzle. Then trade this sheet to solve someone's puzzler.

Clues ACROSS

_____

_____

_____

_____

_____

Clues DOWN

_____

_____

_____

_____

_____

Nonfiction Assessment Record

Book Title: *A Way with Words*

Student _____   Date _____

Say, *Read pages 4 and 5 silently.* Ask, *Why is communication very important to humans?*	Did the student understand how much we rely on communication in a variety of forms? (Learning Outcome 1) ☐
Say, *Read pages 6 and 7 silently.* Ask, *What does the larynx do to help us produce sounds?*	Did the student display an understanding of the role of the larynx? (Purpose for Reading 1) ☐
Say, *Read the time line on pages 8 and 9.* Ask, *Can you put the following child's language development events into the correct order? short sentences; 1,000 words; some nouns*	Was the student able to use the language development time line to correctly sequence these events? (Critical Thinking 1) ☐
Say, *Read pages 12 through 15 silently.* Ask, *Do you think there should be only one world language? Why/Why not?*	Was the student able to form and justify an appropriate opinion? (Critical Thinking 2) ☐
Ask, *Why does the speech of some people from different regions who speak the same language sound quite different?*	Did the student understand the influences of dialect and accent? (Learning Outcome 3) ☐
Say, *Read pages 16 through 19 silently.* Ask, *If you traveled back 1,000 years, why would communication be difficult?*	Did the student display an understanding of the changing nature of language? (Purpose for Reading 2) ☐
Ask, *Why was the development of the printing press very important?*	Could the student form an appropriate generalization? (Learning Outcome 1) ☐
Say, *Read pages 22 and 23 silently.* Ask, *How has technology changed written language?*	Did the student mention "shortening of words" or something similar? (Purpose for Reading 3) ☐

Student Book Notes—*Ancient China*

Synopsis

Ancient China features the history and cultural development of China. The text includes the contributions of the major dynasties and highlights the defense strategies used to keep China safe. Chinese contributions to the rest of the world are featured throughout the book.

Vocabulary Development
acupuncture, ancestor, artisan, calligraphy, class, dynasty, embroider, generation, Silk Road, terra-cotta
Challenges in the Text
historical perspective
Cross-Curricular Connections
social studies—culture, history

Learning Outcomes

Students will:

1. state how the people of China developed their own way of life.
2. recall at least two reasons why ancient Chinese were able to protect themselves.
3. outline advances made by the Chinese in the field of writing.

For Independent Readers

Provide these questions before students read the text:

• What is the only human-built structure visible from space?
• What was the Silk Road?
• Why did China become important to European people?
• How has life changed in China?

Visual Elements

Students have the opportunity to:

1. gain information from a map with captioned text.
2. read and interpret gatefold pages.
3. view a procedural diagram.
4. read a time line.

Purposes for Reading

Possible choices include:

1. to learn about the major dynasties of ancient China.
2. to learn about some customs of ancient China.
3. to learn about some inventions of the ancient Chinese.

Critical Thinking

Students have the opportunity to:

1. form generalizations about family life in ancient China.
2. form opinions about the hierarchy in ancient China.
3. summarize significant information using heightened language.

Special Features

• Read "Time Link" and discover a delicious accident.
• What is a silent army? Read "Profile" to find out.
• Check out "In Focus" to see who wrote about China 700 years ago.

Guiding Learning

Before Reading

Ask, *Why is it important to learn about the history of other countries?* and discuss ideas. Highlight the importance of a historical perspective in broadening understanding and learning more about ourselves.

During Reading

Key text to guide:

Pages 4–5: Read aloud these pages. Discuss how isolation led to a unique cultural development. Ask, *Why did the people settle along the three great rivers?*

Pages 6–7: Explain the concept of dynasties to students, using the glossary entry. Then share read these pages. Challenge students to state their views on the ranking of society. Ask, *Why do you think scholars were highly respected?*

Pages 8–13: Provide the following questions and then, if appropriate, have students read these pages independently to answer: *What was family life like for the ancient Chinese? What sorts of clothing did they wear? How did they celebrate good times?* (Share read with students needing support.) Have students recall what they have learned. Together, reread any sections that require clarification.

Pages 14–19: Either share read or have students read these pages independently. Discuss the importance of the Great Wall, and then help students read and interpret the dynasty time line. Reread page 18 and ask students to speculate why the terra-cotta statues were constructed.

Pages 20–23: Say, *Read to the end of page 23. Find out how the Chinese worked to develop trade within China and with other lands.* When students have finished, highlight the Silk Road's importance.

Pages 24–27: Have students read these pages and then discuss the contributions to writing, medicine, and learning made by the ancient Chinese.

Pages 28–29: Say, *The ancient Chinese were very good at finding practical solutions to many problems. Read to the end of page 29 and discover what some of these were.* When students have finished, discuss the ingenuity of these solutions.

After Reading

Responding: Challenge students to state and discuss ways in which the influence of ancient China is evident in modern times.

Thinking Activity Master 2
Did You Know? Summarizing Significant Information

Discuss how authors sometimes write information as answers to the question "Did You Know?" Talk about the use of heightened language, and how these statements are used to highlight an interesting fact. Demonstrate using some examples and then have students complete the activity.

www.rigbyinfoquest.com
Zone: People & Places
Link: Ancient China

Students can research answers on the site:

1. How do we know about art in ancient China?
2. How did people make bronze objects?
3. Why were horses respected in China?
4. What did people do for fun in ancient China?
5. How were kites first used?

Learning Activities

Students can complete activities on the site:

- Put together a time line.
- Put together a jigsaw puzzle and list the things you can see.

SITESEEING PEOPLE & PLACES

Why were horses respected in China?
Visit **www.rigbyinfoquest.com**
for more about ANCIENT CHINA.

Did You Know?

Name _____ Date _____

Use the index in *Ancient China* to find information and then reread about the topics below. Write an exciting "Did You Know?" fact for each topic.

          1. Scholars   3. Great Wall   5. Inventions

          2. Silk Road   4. Dynasties   6. Emperors

1.

2.

3.

Ancient China

4.

5.

6.

Nonfiction Assessment Record

Book Title: *Ancient China*

Student _____ Date _____

Say, *Read pages 4 and 5 silently.* Ask, *What is the main reason why the people of China developed their own way of life?*	Did the student understand the significance of China's isolation? (Learning Outcome 1)	☐
Say, *Read pages 6 and 7 silently.* Ask, *Why were some people in China more respected than others?*	Did the student understand certain professions were more highly prized than others? (Critical Thinking 2)	☐
Say, *Read pages 8 and 9 silently.* Ask, *How was family life in ancient China different from your own?*	Could the student state two or three differences? (Critical Thinking 1)	☐
Ask, *Why do many Chinese people state their family name first?*	Did the student understand the importance of family? (Purpose for Reading 2)	☐
Say, *Read pages 14 through 19 silently.* Ask, *What are two reasons why the ancient Chinese were able to protect themselves?*	Did the student specify the Great Wall and the superiority of the warriors? (Learning Outcome 2)	☐
Ask, *When did the first dynasty begin, and what was the last dynasty called?*	Did the student use the time line to give the correct answers? (Purpose for Reading 1)	☐
Say, *Read pages 24 and 25 silently.* Ask, *In what ways were the Chinese well ahead of the Europeans in writing?*	Did the student mention papermaking and/or printing? (Learning Outcome 3)	☐
Say, *Read pages 28 and 29 silently.* Ask, *Which three inventions mentioned in these pages do you think were the most important? Why?*	Did the student specify and justify three different inventions from these pages? (Purpose for Reading 3)	☐

Student Book Notes—*Cell City*

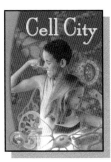

Synopsis

Cell City explores the nature and functions of human cells. The book highlights the main structures in the body and contains a series of useful tips to help keep the body healthy.

Vocabulary Development
bacteria, carbohydrate, enzyme, intestine, melanin, mineral, nutrient, organ, pigment, tissue, vertebrae, vitamin

Challenges in the Text
technical vocabulary

Cross-Curricular Connections
health; physical education

Learning Outcomes

Students will:

1. be able to state the main functions of a cell.
2. display an understanding of the role of the nervous system.
3. explain how the lungs work.

For Independent Readers

Provide these questions before students read the text:

• What are cells, and how many of them do we have in our bodies?
• What different actions do cells do?
• Why do we usually feel pain when we injure ourselves?
• Why are there different skin colors?

Visual Elements

Students have the opportunity to:

1. gain information from a variety of diagrams and photographs.
2. view cross-sectional and cutaway diagrams.
3. read and interpret a diagram with labels.

Purposes for Reading

Possible choices include:

1. to learn about the major types of cells in the human body.
2. to learn how we can keep ourselves healthy.
3. to learn how the major organs of the body function.

Critical Thinking

Students have the opportunity to:

1. summarize information about how the brain functions.
2. form generalizations about the relative importance of the five senses.
3. locate and record important information in the form of a chart.

Special Features

• Read "Try This!" and find out how to improve your fitness.
• Who invented the first hair conditioner? Check out "Fast Facts" to find out.
• See if Kyle can get fit for a sports day. Read about his efforts in "My Diary."

Guiding Learning

Before Reading

Invite students to help list what they know about cells. Prompt with questions such as *What are cells? What different kinds are there? What does each kind of cell do?*

During Reading

Key text to guide:

Pages 4–5: Share read these pages. Discuss the different kinds of cells and their functions. Highlight the "Health Tip" and tell students to watch for these throughout the rest of the book.

Pages 6–11: If possible, have students read independently to the end of page 11 after you first pose the following questions: *Why is learning early in life very important? What is the function of the spinal cord? How does the sense of taste work?* When students have finished, discuss their responses to these questions. Ask, *Which of the five senses do you think is the most important?*

Pages 12–15: Have students read these pages. Help them interpret each of the diagrams. Discuss the way bones and muscles work together to enable us to move. Help students understand that some bones, such as the rib cage and skull, are present to protect vital organs.

Pages 16–19: Say, *Our heart and lungs are two very important organs. Read to the end of page 19 and find out how they work and how we can take care of them.* (Share read with students needing support.) Discuss the health tips and how each of these organs functions.

Pages 20–25: Share read pages 20 and 21. Ensure that students understand the diagram and how skin color is determined. Have students finish reading this section. Discuss the reasons many adults no longer have all their teeth.

Pages 26–27: Share read these pages, helping students understand how the digestive system works. Discuss the food pyramid and then invite students to think about their own eating habits.

Pages 28–29: Have students read these pages and then ask, *Why do you think training got much easier for Kyle?*

After Reading

Responding: Have students review what they have learned from reading *Cell City*. Then have students look at the diagram on page 4 and state the purpose of each type of cell.

Thinking Activity Master 3
Cell City Chart: Locating and Recording Important Information

Demonstrate how to use the contents page and index to locate the required information. Read through the activity with students and then have them complete the worksheet.

www.rigbyinfoquest.com
Zone: Science & Technology
Link: Health Science

Students can research answers on the site:

1. What are hormones?
2. What is adrenaline?
3. What do hair and nails have in common?
4. Are taste and smell connected?
5. Why is blood red?
6. What is the immune system?

Learning Activities

Students can complete activities on the site:

- Journey inside the body and see if you can recognize the bones.
- Write your own clues for a *Cell City* crossword puzzle.

What do hair and nails have in common?
Visit www.rigbyinfoquest.com for more about HEALTH SCIENCE.

Cell City Chart

Name _____   Date _____

Use what you've read to summarize important information.

Part of the Body	Function	Keeping Healthy
Teeth	Chewing and grinding food for digestion	Brush and floss teeth at least twice a day.
Bones		
Heart		
Lungs		
Skin		
Muscles		
Brain		

Nonfiction Assessment Record

Book Title: *Cell City*

Student _____   Date _____

Say, *Read pages 4 and 5 silently.* Ask, *What is the main function of a cell?*	Did the student understand that cells turn nutrients into energy? (Learning Outcome 1)	☐
Ask, *Can you name at least four different types of cells?*	Did the student use the information from the diagram? (Purpose for Reading 1)	☐
Say, *Read pages 6 and 7 silently.* Ask, *Why do brain cells need to be connected to one another?*	Did the student indicate that "paths" are needed in order for the brain to function? (Critical Thinking 1)	☐
Say, *Read pages 8 and 9 silently.* Ask, *What is the main function of the nervous system?*	Did the student understand the role of moving messages to and from the brain? (Learning Outcome 2)	☐
Say, *Read pages 10 and 11 silently.* Ask, *Which sense do you think is the most important? Why?*	Could the student articulate and justify an opinion? (Critical Thinking 2)	☐
Say, *Read pages 16 through 19 silently.* Ask, *Why do children's hearts beat faster than those of adults?*	Did the student understand that children are using more energy to grow? (Purpose for Reading 3)	☐
Ask, *What do the lungs do with the air we breathe?*	Could the student recall the correct information? (Learning Outcome 3)	☐
Ask, *Can you recall three "Health Tips" you have read in this book?*	Could the student recall at least three tips presented in the text? (Purpose for Reading 2)	☐

Student Book Notes—*Dynamic Dance*

Synopsis

Dynamic Dance explores the colorful history of various forms of dance and their cultural importance. The book highlights performance dance and the gradual emergence of social dance. The text concludes with a section explaining how everyone, regardless of physical or intellectual ability, can have fun dancing.

Vocabulary Development
apartheid, banquet, choreographer, indigenous, Renaissance period, Romantic period

Challenges in the Text
historical perspective

Cross-Curricular Connections
social studies; fine arts

Learning Outcomes

Students will:

1. display an understanding of the importance of dance.
2. be able to explain the main tasks of a choreographer.
3. display an understanding of the universal nature of folk dance.

For Independent Readers

Provide these questions before students read the text:

- Why do people dance?
- What is the difference between performance and social dancing?
- What do you know about different types of dances?
- What is your favorite type of dance? Why?

Visual Elements

Students have the opportunity to:

1. view a range of illustrations and photographs.
2. read diary entries with accompanying illustrations.
3. view double-page spreads.

Purposes for Reading

Possible choices include:

1. to learn about the historical beginnings of dance.
2. to learn about different types of dance.
3. to learn about ways dance is becoming available to everyone.

Critical Thinking

Students have the opportunity to:

1. sequence the main steps in the development of ballet.
2. compare and contrast performance and social dancing.
3. locate and summarize key facts about dance and dancers.

Special Features

- Who dances well in rubber boots? Discover the answer with "In Focus."
- What's a Lindy hop? Turn to "Fast Facts" and find out.
- All people can enjoy dancing. Read "Profile" and find out more.

Guiding Learning

Before Reading

Read the title and allow time for students to browse the illustrations. Ask, *How many different kinds of dance did you find? Why do you think dance is very popular throughout the world?* Discuss responses.

During Reading

Key text to guide:

Pages 4–7: Read these pages to students. Discuss the different reasons people dance. Help students understand the cultural significance of dance throughout the world.

Pages 8–9: Say, *Read to the end of page 9 and find out how folk dancing developed.* When students have finished, highlight the importance of folk dance as a way of building togetherness and community spirit.

Pages 10–15: Say, *Read to the end of page 15 and find out how ballet dancing developed.* (Share read with students needing support.) When students have finished, talk about the developments in clothing and the rise of women stars. Reread the interview. Challenge students to discuss the teasing that went on at school.

Pages 16–19: Have students read these pages to find out how modern dance developed, and how it is different from the more traditional ballet style. When students have finished, ensure they understand the role of the choreographer.

Pages 20–21: Ask, *What do you think gumboots are, and why would people dance wearing them?* Have students read these pages and help them understand the unique way the miners were trying to withstand appalling conditions.

Pages 22–27: Tell students to read these pages and find out how dance developed in the 20th century. When students have finished, review the way dance has developed, ensuring they understand that each generation creates its own unique style.

Pages 28–29: Read these pages to students and highlight the fact that everyone, regardless of disabilities, can take part in some form of dance.

After Reading

Responding: Review students' new understanding of differences between performance and social dance. Ask, *How do you think dance might change by the time you are your parents' age?*

Thinking Activity Master 4
Dance and Dancers: Locating and Summarizing Key Facts

Review use of the contents page, index, and glossary to locate specific information. Hand out the worksheets and explain that students are to write the most important fact for each of the topics. Point out to students that the first one is done for them.

www.rigbyinfoquest.com
Zone: Art & Entertainment
Link: Dance

Students can research answers on the site:

1. What is street dance?
2. When did rap music become popular?
3. What does a choreographer do?
4. How are dances choreographed?
5. What happens before a performance?
6. What happens at a performance?

Learning Activities

Students can complete activities on the site:

- Make your own glossary by typing definitions for the words.
- Write clues for the *Dynamic Dance* crossword puzzle.

How are dances choreographed?
Visit www.rigbyinfoquest.com
for more about DANCE.

Dance and Dancers

Name _____ Date _____

Revisit information in *Dynamic Dance* to summarize the most important fact about each topic.

Topic	Key Information
Gumboot dancing	This was the only way for Black African miners to communicate for months at a time.
Elvis Presley	
Folk dances	
The Charleston	
Ruth St. Denis and Ted Shawn	
Choreographer	
Anna Pavlova	
Dance marathons	
Touch Compass Dance Trust	
Isadora Duncan	

Nonfiction Assessment Record

Book Title: *Dynamic Dance*

Student _____   Date _____

Say, *Read pages 4 through 7 silently.* Ask, *What are two different things that dance is able to do?*	Did the student say "communicate stories and emotions" or their equivalents? (Learning Outcome 1)	☐
Ask, *How did some early dances develop?*	Did the student mention "as part of culture"? (Purpose for Reading 1)	☐
Say, *Read pages 8 and 9 silently.* Ask, *Why can the same folk dance appear in many different countries?*	Did the student understand that people took their dances with them when they emigrated? (Learning Outcome 3)	☐
Say, *Read pages 10 through 13 silently.* Ask, *How has ballet dancing changed over time?*	Could the student sequence the main changes in ballet? (Critical Thinking 1)	☐
Say, *Read pages 18 and 19 silently.* Ask, *What are the main tasks of a choreographer?*	Did the student use the text information and/or the glossary to explain the main tasks? (Learning Outcome 2)	☐
Say, *Read pages 28 and 29 silently.* Ask, *What is special about the Touch Compass Dance Trust?*	Did the student indicate "catering for people with disabilities"? (Purpose for Reading 3)	☐
Ask, *Can you recall at least three different types of dance from this book?*	Could the student recall at least three different types of dance from the book? (Purpose for Reading 2)	☐
Ask, *What is the main difference between performance and social dance?*	Did the student understand that one involves an audience, while the other is for personal fun or recreation? (Critical Thinking 2)	☐

Student Book Notes—*Eye on the Ball*

Synopsis

Eye on the Ball takes a close look at sports that involve the use of a ball. The book traces the history and development of these sports, and it highlights some famous stars who have played them.

Vocabulary Development
archaeology, historian, media, official, publicity, sponsor, synthetic
Challenges in the Text
historical perspective
Cross-Curricular Connections
social studies—culture; physical education

Learning Outcomes

Students will:

1. display an understanding of the difference between amateur and professional sports.
2. state how technology has influenced many ball sports.
3. recall the main features of a specific sport.

For Independent Readers

Provide these questions before students read the text:

- Why are sports involving balls popular?
- What are the differences between American and British football?
- What is your favorite ball sport?
- Which ball sports star do you most admire? Why?

Visual Elements

Students have the opportunity to:

1. gain information from a variety of illustrations and photographs.
2. interpret a diagram with leadered text.
3. read double-page spreads.
4. view a gatefold section.

Purposes for Reading

Possible choices include:

1. to learn historical origins of ball sports.
2. to learn how some sports have developed from others.
3. to continue effectively using a variety of text organizers.

Critical Thinking

Students have the opportunity to:

1. compare and contrast a variety of sports involving balls.
2. form and justify opinions about sports that are less familiar to them.
3. use information in the text to invent a new ball game.

Special Features

- Check out "Time Link" to learn about the oldest sport in North America.
- "In the News" features the retirement of a top tennis star. See who she is.
- Read the "Profile" of one of the most famous quarterbacks in football.
- Throughout the book, "Fast Facts" presents the basics about many sports.

Guiding Learning
Before Reading
Together with students, brainstorm a list of favorite ball sports. Ask, *What is similar about some of these sports? What are some differences?* Amend this list as the reading of the book proceeds.

During Reading
Key text to guide:

Pages 4–5: Have students read page 4 independently. Discuss the different reasons for the invention of ball sports. Share read page 5. Ask, *Can you think of any modern sports similar to lacrosse?* If appropriate, add lacrosse to the list from the "Before Reading" session.

Pages 6–7: Share read these pages. Invite students to look up the glossary entries. Ask, *Why do you think many people now have sports-related jobs?* Help students understand the impact of mass media and professionalism.

Pages 8–11: Say, *Read to the end of page 11 to find out how tennis and badminton are similar and different.* Discuss how the aims are similar but the rules are somewhat different.

Pages 12–13: Have students read these pages and discuss why bowling is popular around the world. (It's a simple game and suitable for most age groups.)

Pages 14–21: Say, *Read to the end of page 21 to find out how rugby and American football developed.* (Share read with students needing more support.) Then challenge students to state how these sports developed and discuss the similarities and differences in these sports.

Pages 22–25: Ask, *What sports involve bats and balls?* Have students read to the end of page 24 and discuss these sports. Read page 25 to students. Highlight the fact that a cricket game can last five days and still not have a result!

Pages 26–29: Say, *Read to the end of page 29. Find out the differences between basketball and netball and between field and ice hockey.* Then have students share their findings.

After Reading
Responding: Review and amend the list started in the "Before Reading" session. Ask, *What is similar about all these sports?*

Thinking Activity Master 5
A New Ball Sport: Using Text Information
Have students find all the "Fast Facts" in the book. Discuss the layout and content, and what else could be included to help explain each game more fully. Tell students that they are to invent a new ball game. Review how they can use the contents page, glossary, and index to gather ideas.

www.rigbyinfoquest.com
Zone: Sports & Adventure
Link: Ball Games
Students can research answers on the site:
1. How do people play table tennis?
2. What is curling on keen or "swingy" ice?
3. What is a footbag?
4. What is juggling?
5. How do people play golf?
6. How did the game of golf begin?

Learning Activities
Students can complete activities on the site:
- Play a tennis game against the computer.
- Use the pictures to write directions for making a footbag.

How do people play table tennis?
Visit www.rigbyinfoquest.com
for more about BALL GAMES.

A New Ball Sport

Name _____   Date _____

Use what you've read in *Eye on the Ball* to invent a ball game. Write its details.

Name of the Sport: . . . .

Number of Players: . . . .

Aim of the Game: . . . .

. . . .

. . . .

. . . .

Equipment Needed: . . . .

. . . .

. . . .

. . . .

Rules of the Game: . . . .

. . . .

. . . .

. . . .

. . . .

. . . .

. . . .

. . . .

Nonfiction Assessment Record

Book Title: *Eye on the Ball*

Student _____   Date _____

Say, *Read pages 6 and 7 silently.* Ask, *How could you use this book to find out what* media *means?*	Did the student show or talk about using the glossary? (Purpose for Reading 3) ☐
Ask, *What is the main difference between professional and amateur sports?*	Did the student understand that professionals are paid to train and play? (Learning Outcome 1) ☐
Say, *Read pages 8 and 9 silently.* Ask, *What are two ways tennis has changed since the 1100s?*	Did the student specify two pieces of information from these pages? (Purpose for Reading 1) ☐
Say, *Read pages 14 through 19 silently.* Ask, *How did the game of rugby develop from soccer?*	Did the student understand that someone picked up the ball and ran with it? (Purpose for Reading 3) ☐
Ask, *What is one similarity and one difference between rugby and soccer?*	Could the student provide one similarity and one difference? (Critical Thinking 1) ☐
Say, *Think about the whole book.* Ask, *What are two ways technology has changed ball sports?*	Did the student indicate improved equipment, surfaces, and/or media coverage? (Learning Outcome 2) ☐
Ask, *Can you tell me the aim and equipment used in one sport from this book?*	Could the student recall the correct information? (Learning Outcome 3) ☐
Say, *Think of a sport in the book that is new to you.* Ask, *Would you like to try playing that sport? Why/Why not?*	Could the student form and justify an opinion? (Critical Thinking 2) ☐

Student Book Notes—*Frontiers of Technology*

Synopsis

Frontiers of Technology explores the ways technology has changed the lives of ordinary people. It highlights changes in our daily lives, medical science, and travel. The book features some predictions from the past and invites students to imagine future advances.

Vocabulary Development
acceleration force, amputee, genetically engineered, infectious, intranet, levitate, microchip, molecule, mutation, prosthetic, virtual reality

Challenges in the Text
technical vocabulary

Cross-Curricular Connections
technology; social studies; ecology

Learning Outcomes

Students will:

1. recall ways in which computers have changed education.
2. display an understanding of why it's important to protect natural resources.
3. explain ways robots can be useful.

For Independent Readers

Provide these questions before students read the text:

- How has technology affected home life?
- How has technology changed school life?
- Do you think technology will someday cure all diseases?
- What would you like to invent?

Visual Elements

Students have the opportunity to:

1. use cutaway diagrams with numbered text.
2. view and read captioned illustrations.
3. interpret photographs and illustrations.
4. read double-page spreads.

Purposes for Reading

Possible choices include:

1. to learn some ways technology has changed people's lives.
2. to learn about some technological advances in travel.
3. to learn about some advances in medical science.

Critical Thinking

Students have the opportunity to:

1. form generalizations about predictions made in the 20th century.
2. form and justify opinions about genetic research.
3. use text information to make predictions about future technological advances.

Special Features

- "Techtalk" presents wireless technology.
- "Profile" will help you see if you have what it takes to be a good scientist.
- Read "What's Your Opinion?" and think about genetic research.
- What would you do with an IBOT? "Fast Facts" gives you a clue.

Guiding Learning

Before Reading

Help students understand that technology is the practical application of science. Have students brainstorm examples of technology in their own homes. Ask, *What three examples of technology would you most miss if they were taken away? Why?*

During Reading

Key text to guide:

Pages 4–5: Share read these pages. Talk about some of the predictions that didn't come true. Discuss reasons why people may have made these predictions.

Pages 6–11: Have students read page 6. Then share read the text at the bottom across the spread. Ask, *Which of these possibilities do you think will become a reality?* Then ask, *How has technology made learning easier?* Have students read pages 8 and 9 and discuss. Share read pages 10 and 11. Help students understand virtual reality. Challenge students to recall an example of technology from home, school, and the world of entertainment.

Pages 12–15: Read page 12 to students. Discuss DNA. Then ask, *What qualities are needed to be a good scientist?* Share read the interview on page 13 and discuss Susan Stasiuk's work. Read pages 14 and 15 to students. Discuss the content and invite students to offer and justify opinions about the worth of genetic research.

Pages 16–17: Say, *Read pages 16 and 17 to find out how technology is helping people with physical disabilities.* Discuss how important these advances are.

Pages 18–19: Have students read these pages and discuss the benefits of robots. Invite students to offer opinions on the question posed on page 19.

Pages 20–25: Say, *Read to the end of page 25 to find out about advances in travel around town, around the world, and beyond.* (Share read with students needing support.) Students can discuss what they find out.

Pages 26–29: Share read these pages and then discuss the importance of protecting the Earth's natural resources.

After Reading

Responding: Have students use the index to locate and reread about an example of technology. Challenge them to state the technology's benefits.

Thinking Activity Master 6

Into the Future: Making Predictions

Have students reread pages 28 and 29. Ask, *What new inventions do you think people will use in the future?* Give students time to discuss their ideas before reading through the activity sheet with you.

www.rigbyinfoquest.com

Zone: Science & Technology
Link: Transportation Technology

Students can research answers on the site:

1. What are alternative fuels?
2. How might an airplane fly like a helicopter?
3. What are some future plans for the tiltrotor?
4. What is a "mood car"?

Learning Activities

Students can complete activities on the site:

- Create your own robotic scooter.
- Write about future technology you would like.

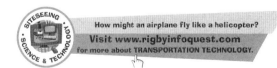

SITESEEING • SCIENCE & TECHNOLOGY

How might an airplane fly like a helicopter?
Visit www.rigbyinfoquest.com
for more about TRANSPORTATION TECHNOLOGY.

Into the Future

Name _____   Date _____

What do you think technology will have produced 100 years from now?

Future Homes

Schools of the Future

Entertainment

Travel

Frontiers of Technology

Medical Science

The Environment

Nonfiction Assessment Record

Book Title: *Frontiers of Technology*

Student _____   Date _____

Say, *Read pages 4 and 5 silently.* Ask, *Why do you think some predictions didn't come true?*	Did the student display understanding the difficulty of making predictions? (Critical Thinking 1)	☐
Say, *Read pages 6 and 7 silently.* Ask, *How have inventions in the home changed people's lives?*	Did the student indicate that these inventions have made life easier? (Purpose for Reading 1)	☐
Say, *Read pages 8 and 9 silently.* Ask, *What are the main benefits of computers in schools?*	Did the student say "fun" or "making learning easier"? (Learning Outcome 1)	☐
Say, *Read pages 14 and 15 silently.* Ask, *Do you think genetic research is a good idea? Why?*	Was the student able to articulate and justify a position? (Critical Thinking 2)	☐
Say, *Read pages 16 and 17 silently.* Ask, *Why was the development of prosthetic limbs important?*	Did the student indicate that it enabled people with disabilities to do much more? (Purpose for Reading 3)	☐
Say, *Read pages 18 and 19 silently.* Ask, *What are three ways robots will be able to help in the future?*	Did the student offer at least three examples from these pages? (Learning Outcome 3)	☐
Say, *Read pages 22 and 23 silently.* Ask, *Why will trains be able to travel at much higher speeds in the future?*	Did the student understand that levitation would minimize friction? (Purpose for Reading 2)	☐
Say, *Read pages 26 and 27 silently.* Ask, *How do some inventors work towards a "green" future?*	Did the student indicate "combining old products with modern methods"? (Learning Outcome 2)	☐

Student Book Notes—*Getting Together*

Synopsis

Getting Together explores some of the reasons people form friendships and join clubs and organized groups. The book highlights both the ways in which people conform or express themselves through fashion and the rights and responsibilities of belonging to a society or nation.

Vocabulary Development
ballot, conform, democracy, extended family, motto, naturalization, nuclear family, peer pressure, society, social science

Challenges in the Text
historical perspective; vocabulary

Cross-Curricular Connections
social studies—citizenship

Learning Outcomes

Students will:

1. display an understanding of why people group together.
2. be able to state the main advantages of being involved in Scouts or Guides.
3. recall how people become citizens in a democratic society.

For Independent Readers

Provide these questions before students read the text:

- Why do most people like to be around others that are like them?
- How did you choose your best friend?
- If you could form your own club, what would it be?
- How did Scouting begin?

Visual Elements

Students have the opportunity to:

1. view cartoon illustrations.
2. read thought bubbles.
3. read and interpret photographs and illustrations.
4. view double-page spreads.

Purposes for Reading

Possible choices include:

1. to learn about some different types of clubs and groups.
2. to learn about the main reasons people form friendships.
3. to learn about some of the positive and negative effects of conforming.

Critical Thinking

Students have the opportunity to:

1. form and justify opinions about the use of school uniforms.
2. form generalizations about the reasons people wear particular clothes.
3. summarize information in order to imagine a new type of club.

Special Features

- Turn to "Fast Facts" and find some fascinating information about flags.
- Have some fun identifying uniforms. "Fact Finder" supplies the clues.
- What do you think about school uniforms? Read "What's Your Opinion?" and have your say.
- Women didn't always wear pants. Read "In Focus" and find out why.

Guiding Learning

Before Reading

Read the title to students and discuss the cover photograph. Ask, *Do you think these people are friends? Why? Think about your own best friend. In what ways are he or she and you similar and different?*

During Reading

Key text to guide:

Pages 4–5: Read these pages to students. Ask, *What are some of the reasons people enjoy the company of others?* Discuss the term "social animals."

Pages 6–7: Say, *Read pages 6 and 7 and find out the main reason people form friendships.* Challenge students to think about their own friends and how the "similarity principle" applies to them.

Pages 8–14: Have students read these pages independently. Provide guidelines similar to the following: *How do we know people belong to a particular group? What is special about the Olympic flag?* Challenge students to name all the uniforms on pages 12 and 13. When students have finished, talk about some of the more obvious outward signs of belonging to a group.

Pages 15–19: Share read page 15. Invite students to debate the issue of school uniforms. Then say, *Read to the end of page 19 and find out how fashion has changed over the years.* Highlight the fashion restrictions in the past based on gender and social class.

Pages 20–21: Have students read these pages independently and discuss the advantages of belonging to one of these groups.

Pages 22–25: Have students read about each of the clubs on these pages. Then have them specify two or three they would like to try and tell why.

Pages 26–27: Ask, *What is a democracy? How do people become citizens in a democratic country?* Have students articulate their ideas, then read these pages, and discuss.

Pages 28–29: Ask, *When is it good to follow what other people do, and when is it bad? How can you help yourself decide what to do?* Have students read these pages and talk about conformity and peer pressure.

After Reading

Responding: Invite students to think about their own behavior and peer pressure. Talk about how caring and trusted adults can often help.

Thinking Activity Master 7

My Own Club: Summarizing Information

Have students think about a club they would like to create. Remind them that most clubs have rules, rights, and responsibilities. Then have students, either individually or in pairs, complete the activity.

www.rigbyinfoquest.com

Zone: People & Places

Link: Identity

Students can research answers on the site:

1. How have hair fashions changed over time?
2. How were fashion trends set in the past?
3. How can hair fashions identify a person's culture or beliefs?
4. Why are customs important?

Learning Activities

Students can complete activities on the site:

- Think about a question and write two opinions.
- Identify some of the differences between Western and Eastern cultures.

How have hair fashions changed over time?
Visit www.rigbyinfoquest.com
for more about IDENTITY.

My Own Club

Name _____   Date _____

Imagine and describe a club that you would like to create.

Club Name _____

Membership (who may join) _____

_____

_____

Club Rules _____

_____

_____

_____

Club Activities _____

_____

_____

_____

Club Motto _____

+---+
| **Club Flag** |
| |
| |
| |
| |
| |
| |
+---+

Nonfiction Assessment Record

Book Title: *Getting Together*

Student _____   Date _____

Say, *Read pages 4 and 5 silently.* Ask, *What are two reasons people like to join together?*	Could the student recall at least two different examples from these pages? (Learning Outcome 1)	☐
Say, *Read pages 6 and 7 silently.* Ask, *What is the main reason why people choose their friends?*	Did the student mention the "similarity principle"? (Purpose for Reading 2)	☐
Say, *Read page 15 silently.* Ask, *Do you think school uniforms are a good idea? Why/Why not?*	Was the student able to state and justify an opinion? (Critical Thinking 1)	☐
Say, *Read pages 16 and 17 silently.* Ask, *Why do groups of people often wear similar types of clothes?*	Did the student understand the need for identification with a particular group? (Critical Thinking 2)	☐
Say, *Read pages 20 and 21 silently.* Ask, *What are two advantages of belonging to Scouts or Guides?*	Was the student able to state at least two different advantages? (Learning Outcome 2)	☐
Say, *Read pages 22 through 25 silently.* Ask, *Which of these clubs would you like to try, and why?*	Was the student able to choose at least one club and give reasons for that choice? (Purpose for Reading 1)	☐
Say, *Read pages 26 and 27 silently.* Ask, *What are two ways people become citizens in a democratic country?*	Did the student specify birth and naturalization? (Learning Outcome 3)	☐
Say, *Read pages 28 and 29 silently.* Ask, *What is one positive and one negative effect of conforming?*	Did the student offer at least one positive and one negative effect? (Purpose for Reading 3)	☐

Student Book Notes—*Good Sports*

Synopsis

Good Sports highlights some of the accomplishments of famous athletes throughout the world. It explores the backgrounds of these athletes, emphasizing their hard work and dedication. The book also features the efforts and accomplishments of athletes with handicaps.

Vocabulary Development
agility, disqualify, motivation, physiology, podium, rookie, self-esteem, sponsor
Challenges in the Text
time line; biographies
Cross-Curricular Connections
physical education; health

Learning Outcomes

Students will:
1. display an understanding of why Pelé is considered the greatest soccer player.
2. be able to state why Shannon Miller's accomplishments are special.
3. state ways we can all become better at our chosen sports.

For Independent Readers

Provide these questions before students read the text:
- What are some of the qualities required to be a top athlete?
- Who is your favorite athlete? Why?
- What special challenges do athletes with handicaps face?
- In which sport would you like to improve your skills?

Visual Elements

Students have the opportunity to:
1. read and interpret a map with a key.
2. read and interpret a time line.
3. interpret photographs and illustrations.
4. view double-page spreads.

Purposes for Reading

Possible choices include:
1. to learn about the qualities required to become a world-class athlete.
2. to learn about the challenges facing paraplegic athletes.
3. to learn about the function and format of bibliographies.

Critical Thinking

Students have the opportunity to:
1. locate and summarize information about an athlete.
2. find and sequence important information from a time line.
3. compose, sequence, and summarize information in the form of a profile.

Special Features

- Read "In the News" and get up-to-date with some of the latest sports stories.
- Check out "In Focus" and decide if you could train like Ian Thorpe.
- When did Shannon Miller win her first Olympic gold medal? "Fast Facts" has the answer.

Guiding Learning
Before Reading
Read the title to students. Ask, *What makes a world-class athlete? Do you think some people are just born talented, or do they need to work on their chosen pursuit?*

During Reading
Key text to guide:

Pages 4–5: Share read these pages. Discuss the hard work and training that goes into becoming a sports star.

Pages 6–9: Say, *Read to the end of page 9 and find out why Pelé is considered the best soccer player of all time.* When students have finished, discuss the records set by Pelé and his continuing dedication to the game.

Pages 10–11: Share read these pages. Ask, *In what way are Mia Hamm and Walter Payton similar?*

Pages 12–15: Have students talk about some of the challenges facing athletes with handicaps. Then have them read to the end of page 15. Ask, *How did Tracey Ferguson overcome her lack of size?* Help students understand how development of some skills and abilities can compensate for a lack of others.

Pages 16–17: Have students read these pages independently. Then ask, *What did Bart Bunting do in order to succeed at the highest level?*

Pages 18–21: Have students read the body text on these pages. Then discuss the diary entries. Ask, *What does this tell you about Ian Thorpe's dedication?* Turn to the career time line and have students locate the dates of specific events.

Pages 22–23: Have students read these pages independently. Ask, *Do you think "Eric the Eel's" performance was as important as that of Mark Spitz or Shane Gould? Why/Why not?*

Pages 24–27: Say, *Read to the end of page 27 and find out what made Shannon Miller special.* Then talk about how, like the other athletes in the book, Shannon Miller continues to contribute to her sport.

Pages 28–29: Have students read these pages and talk about how they can be more successful at playing their chosen sports.

After Reading
Responding: Turn to the bibliography on page 31. Highlight how each entry is presented: author, title, publisher, and date. Discuss the functions of a bibliography. (It shows which publications the author used and provides a list for further reading.)

Thinking Activity Master 8
My Favorite Athlete: Composing, Sequencing, and Summarizing Information
Have students choose a famous athlete and complete a profile for that person. Alternatively, students could choose one of the athletes other than Ian Thorpe from the book.

www.rigbyinfoquest.com
Zone: Sports & Adventure
Link: Sports
Students can research answers on the site:
1. What are the different swimming strokes?
2. What swimming events are in the Olympic Games?
3. How big is an Olympic pool?
4. What is a triathlon?
5. What is a duathlon?

Learning Activities
Students can complete activities on the site:
- Write a newspaper article about a sporting event.
- Write a schedule for practicing a sport.

What are the different swimming strokes?
Visit www.rigbyinfoquest.com
for more about SPORTS.

My Favorite Athlete

Name _____   Date _____

Choose an athlete and complete a time line about that person's life.

My favorite athlete is _____

A Time Line of Important Events

Date   Event

_____   _____

                _____

_____   _____

                _____

_____   _____

                _____

_____   _____

                _____

(You can continue on the back.)

My favorite athlete's most important accomplishment was _____

_____

_____

I chose this person as my favorite athlete because _____

_____

_____

Nonfiction Assessment Record

Book Title: *Good Sports*

Student _____   Date _____

Say, *Read pages 6 through 9 silently.* Ask, *Why is Pelé still considered the greatest soccer player?*	Did the student understand the significance of the records Pelé holds? (Learning Outcome 1)	☐
Say, *Read pages 12 through 15 silently.* Ask, *Can you summarize how Tracey Ferguson feels about basketball?*	Did the student understand that the sport has meant much more than just medals to her? (Critical Thinking 1)	☐
Ask, *How did Tracey Ferguson make up for her lack of size?*	Did the student mention speed, agility, or expert shooting? (Purpose for Reading 2)	☐
Say, *Look at the time line on pages 20 and 21. Put these events in order: the Olympic Games at Sydney, the Pan Pacific Championships in Japan, the Commonwealth Games in Kuala Lumpur.*	Was the student able to use the time line to put these events in chronological order? (Critical Thinking 2)	☐
Say, *Read pages 24 through 27 silently.* Ask, *What was very special about Shannon Miller's accomplishments?*	Did the student understand how far ahead of her competition she was? (Learning Outcome 2)	☐
Say, *Read pages 28 and 29 silently.* Ask, *How can we all be better at playing our chosen sports?*	Did the student understand the roles of training, enjoyment, and setting goals? (Learning Outcome 3)	☐
Say, *Look at the bibliography on page 31.* Ask, *Why do authors sometimes include a bibliography?*	Could the student supply at least one reason for the inclusion of a bibliography? (Purpose for Reading 3)	☐
Ask, *What qualities do most world-class athletes need?*	Did the student mention hard work, training, or dedication? (Purpose for Reading 1)	☐

Student Book Notes—*It's Show Time*

Synopsis

It's Show Time explores the origins of some of the oldest and most loved performing arts. From stilt walkers and street performers to the modern circus, the book outlines what different artists have to offer and why they do what they do. The book includes a section on how young people can become circus performers.

Vocabulary Development
acrobatics, cast, comedian, improvise, minstrel, prop, puppeteer, slapstick, tip, troupe
Challenges in the Text
map with text; interview format
Cross-Curricular Connections
social studies—culture

Learning Outcomes

Students will:

1. be able to state the main reasons why people have traditionally used stilts.
2. understand the importance of nontraditional circuses.
3. recall some of the main skills required to be a clown.

For Independent Readers

Provide these questions before students read the text:

- Have you ever been to a circus? What was the most exciting act?
- Who were Punch and Judy?
- What does a ringmaster do?
- Would you like to work in a circus? What would you do?

Visual Elements

Students have the opportunity to:

1. read and interpret a map with accompanying text.
2. read and interpret photographs and illustrations.
3. view double-page spreads.

Purposes for Reading

Possible choices include:

1. to learn about the use of stilts throughout the world.
2. to learn about some roles of different street performers.
3. to learn how young people can train to become performers.

Critical Thinking

Students have the opportunity to:

1. form generalizations about why people like to perform for others.
2. form and justify an opinion about the use of animals in circuses.
3. summarize information in the form of a diary.

Special Features

- Turn to "In Focus" and find out how a professional stilt walker trains.
- Read "What's Your Opinion?" and have your say about circus animals.
- Check out "Profile" to discover how a street kid developed a new kind of circus.
- Read through "My Diary" and learn about what goes on at a circus camp.

Guiding Learning

Before Reading

Read the title to students. Ask, *Why do people like to perform for others? How are live performances different from other types of performances?* Record the students' responses for the After Reading session.

During Reading

Key text to guide:

Pages 4–5: Have students read these pages and discuss some of the traditional reasons people used stilts.

Pages 6–9: Share read pages 6 and 7. Help students locate specific countries and summarize some different uses of stilts. Have students read page 8 independently, and then have them pair up to read the interview. Ask, *What other questions could the interviewer have asked?*

Pages 10–15: Have students read these pages independently. Say, *Read to the end of page 15. Find out about the different kinds of street performers, what they do, and how it all began.* (Share read with students needing support.) Then discuss the variety of street performers and the longevity and attraction of puppet theater.

Pages 16–17: Have students discuss their experiences with circuses and then read these pages independently. Ask, *Should circuses have wild animals? Why/Why not?*

Pages 18–23: Ask, *How do you think circuses could be made better for people with handicaps?* Have students discuss their ideas and then read to the end of page 21. Afterward, have students recall ways in which these different circuses are helping people. Read pages 22 and 23 to students, and then talk about the effort that goes into each show.

Pages 24–25: Have students read these pages independently before talking about how this circus helps children across Australia.

Pages 26–29: Say, *Read to the end of page 29. Find out how children can train to be performers and what it takes to be a clown.* Discuss what students have found out. Then reread the two diary entries and discuss some of the similarities in content.

After Reading

Responding: Review the responses from the Before Reading session. Ask, *Now that you have read the book, how do you now respond to these questions?* Challenge students to justify their points of view.

Thinking Activity Master 9
Circus Camp Diary: Summarizing Information

Review students' understanding of diaries. Emphasize the diary format (chronology, informal language, etc.). Have students imagine they are at circus camp by using information from the book. They are to use their imaginations to write about their day at circus camp.

www.rigbyinfoquest.com
Zone: Art & Entertainment
Link: Puppets

Students can research answers on the site:

1. Where were marionettes invented?
2. How are puppet shows of shadows created?
3. What are two types of hand puppets?
4. How are rod puppets used?
5. What are Bunraku puppets?
6. Where are water puppets a tradition?

Learning Activities

Students can complete activities on the site:

- Create puppets and a scene for a show.
- Unscramble the words to complete the sentences.

SITESEEING • ART & ENTERTAINMENT •

Where were marionettes invented?
Visit **www.rigbyinfoquest.com**
for more about **PUPPETS.**

Circus Camp Diary

Name _____   Date _____

Imagine that you've spent the day at a circus camp. Write about events and how you felt at different times of the day.

Time: _____   _____

_____

_____

_____

Time: _____   _____

_____

_____

_____

Time: _____   _____

_____

_____

_____

Time: _____   _____

_____

_____

_____

Time: _____   _____

_____

_____

_____

(You can continue on the back of this sheet if you need more space.)

Nonfiction Assessment Record

Book Title: *It's Show Time*

Student _____   Date _____

Say, *Read pages 4 and 5 silently.* Ask, *What is the main reason why people long ago used stilts?*	Did the student understand that stilts were necessary to keep feet dry? (Learning Outcome 1) ☐
Say, *Read pages 6 and 7 silently.* Ask, *How is the use of stilts in Japan and Sudan different?*	Could the student understand that one use is to avoid heat and the other to avoid cold? (Purpose for Reading 1) ☐
Say, *Read pages 10 through 15 silently.* Ask, *What are some of the different actions done by street performers?*	Could the student recall at least three different types of street performances? (Purpose for Reading 2) ☐
Say, *Read pages 16 and 17 silently.* Ask, *Do you think wild animals should be used in circuses? Why/Why not?*	Was the student able to articulate and justify a position? (Critical Thinking 2) ☐
Say, *Read pages 18 and 19 silently.* Ask, *Why are circuses like Circus of the Senses important?*	Did the student understand that these circuses cater for people with handicaps? (Learning Outcome 2) ☐
Say, *Read pages 26 and 27 silently.* Ask, *What is the main purpose of a circus camp?*	Did the student say the purpose is to prepare students for all aspects of circus life? (Purpose for Reading 3) ☐
Say, *Read pages 28 and 29 silently.* Ask, *What are some of the main skills required to be a clown?*	Could the student specify at least three different skills? (Learning Outcome 3) ☐
Say, *Think about the whole book.* Ask, *Why do you think people like to perform for others?*	Was the student able to form an appropriate generalization? (Critical Thinking 1) ☐

Student Book Notes—*Lands of Rock*

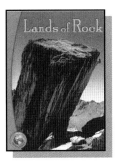

Synopsis

From high mountain peaks to underground caves, the nature of our rocky planet is explored in *Lands of Rock*. The book highlights the importance of rocks to different people, and it focuses on a variety of recreational pursuits in rocky places.

Vocabulary Development

alpine, ascend, badlands, bouldering, canyon, crevasse, descend, geologist, mesa, monolith, paleontologist, pictograph, plateau, summit

Challenges in the Text
biographies; technical language

Cross-Curricular Connections
earth science; social studies

Learning Outcomes

Students will:

1. recall the two main reasons rocks change shape.
2. be able to state why fossils are important.
3. display understanding of the importance of rocky places to different people.

For Independent Readers

Provide these questions before students read the text:

- What are the three main types of rock?
- What can be learned from fossils?
- In what different ways do people use rocks?
- How do rocks change shape?

Visual Elements

Students have the opportunity to:

1. view a variety of photographs and illustrations.
2. interpret a map with a symbol key.
3. read captioned text.
4. read and interpret icon-supported text.

Purposes for Reading

Possible choices include:

1. to learn about some features of canyon country.
2. to learn about some of the recreational opportunities in rocky lands.
3. to learn about some features of underground environments.

Critical Thinking

Students have the opportunity to:

1. form generalizations about why some people have lived in rock dwellings.
2. read and interpret a map with symbols.
3. compose a map and key with symbols.

Special Features

- "My Diary" presents the words of the first person to explore unknown canyons.
- Can you imagine being trapped in an ice cave? Read about courage in "Profile."
- "Try This!" allows you to imagine an adventure in the wilderness.

Guiding Learning

Before Reading

Read the back cover to students, and then have them compile a list of questions they think the book might answer. Keep this list for the After Reading session.

During Reading

Key text to guide:

Pages 4–7: Either share read or read these pages to students. Have students use the glossary when appropriate. Discuss the different reasons rocks are important to a variety of people. Ask, *In what ways do fire and water help shape Earth's surface?*

Pages 8–13: Have students read these pages independently. (Share read with students needing support.) When they've finished, review the map on page 9, ensuring that students understand the use of symbols. Talk about the dangers faced by early explorers of the canyon country. Then challenge students to suggest why the Anasazi Indians lived where they did.

Pages 14–15: Say, *Why are fossils important? Read page 14 to find out.* When students have finished, have them discuss their responses to the question. Then read page 15 to students and discuss.

Pages 16–25: If appropriate, have students read these pages independently. Say, *On the following pages you will find a range of activities that are done in rocky places. Read to the end of page 25 to find out what each activity involves and the ways to make each activity safe.* You may want to have students make notes in point form as they read. When finished, invite students to share and compare their findings.

Pages 26–27: Ask, *How are underground rocks and rock formations different from ones above ground?* Have students read to the end of page 27. Then talk about major features of underground environments.

Pages 28–29: Review any room rules for playing this game. Then provide time for students to have some fun picking up safety tips along a nature-filled hike.

After Reading

Responding: Review the questions from the Before Reading session. Suggest students use available reference materials, including the *Rigby InfoQuest* Web site, to research answers for any remaining questions.

Thinking Activity Master 10
Mapmaking: Composing a Map with a Key and Symbols

Discuss the map and use of symbols on page 9. Tell students that they are to make their own maps, thinking of appropriate symbols to include. They each might choose a map of the whole school, the neighborhood, or home.

www.rigbyinfoquest.com
Zone: Sports & Adventure
Link: Mountain Climbing

Students can research answers on the site:

1. Where are Earth's highest mountains?
2. Where do Sherpas live?
3. Who first climbed the world's highest mountain?
4. How did Sir Edmund Hillary help the Sherpa?
5. How can animals live in mountain areas?

Learning Activities

Students can complete activities on the site:

- Fill in the speech bubbles to write your own comic strip.
- Hike through the wilderness by playing *Survive!*

Mapmaking

Name _____   Date _____

Draw a map of the whole school, a neighborhood, or your home. Use symbols to label different areas. Make a key of these symbols and what they represent.

This is a map of _____

Key

Nonfiction Assessment Record

Book Title: *Lands of Rock*

Student _____   Date _____

Say, *Read pages 4 and 5 silently.* Ask, *Why do geologists and climbers like rocks?*	Did the student understand the different reasons? (Learning Outcome 3)	☐
Say, *Read pages 6 and 7 silently.* Ask, *What are the two main reasons rocks change shape?*	Did the student mention "fiery forces" and "water"? (Learning Outcome 1)	☐
Say, *Read pages 8 and 9 silently.* Ask, *Can you describe some of the features of canyon country?*	Was the student able to recall at least three features? (Purpose for Reading 1)	☐
Ask, *In which state is the Petrified Forest?*	Could the student use the map to locate the information? (Critical Thinking 2)	☐
Say, *Read pages 12 and 13 silently.* Ask, *Why do you think the Anasazi Indians lived in rock dwellings?*	Could the student form and justify an appropriate opinion? (Critical Thinking 1)	☐
Say, *Read pages 14 and 15 silently.* Ask, *Why is the study of fossils important?*	Did the student understand that fossils can tell us about our past? (Learning Outcome 2)	☐
Say, *Read pages 26 and 27 silently.* Ask, *How are stalagmites and stalactites formed?*	Did the student indicate an understanding of the process? (Purpose for Reading 3)	☐
Ask, *Can you recall at least three recreational opportunities highlighted in the book?*	Could the student recall at least three examples? (Purpose for Reading 2)	☐

Student Book Notes—*Matter Splatter!*

Synopsis

Matter Splatter! outlines the three common states of matter, how they differ, and how they can change. The book highlights how matter is used in a variety of ways through mixtures and alloys. It concludes by exploring some of the fascinating properties of plastics and cardboard.

Vocabulary Development

atom, compress, decompose, evaporate, expand, flammable, invisible, mass, molecule, polymer, resin, viscous

Challenges in the Text

technical vocabulary; biography

Cross-Curricular Connections

physical science; technology

Learning Outcomes

Students will:

1. be able to specify the three main states of matter.
2. recall and describe what a solution is.
3. display an understanding of how matter changes.

For Independent Readers

Provide these questions before students read the text:

- Everything in the universe is matter. What is matter?
- Are solids always heavier than liquids?
- There is a fourth state of matter called *plasma*. How is it different?
- How does matter change?

Visual Elements

Students have the opportunity to:

1. gain information from a variety of diagrams and photographs.
2. read and interpret sequenced diagrams.
3. read instructional text with accompanying illustrations.

Purposes for Reading

Possible choices include:

1. to learn or review what matter is.
2. to learn about the different types of matter.
3. to learn how new types of matter are being created.

Critical Thinking

Students have the opportunity to:

1. compare different ways matter changes.
2. form and justify opinions about the use of plastics.
3. use text features to locate and record important information.

Special Features

- Read "Profile" and discover who first split the atom and what he found inside.
- Why would anyone build a cardboard boat? Read "In the News" to find out.
- Balloons can be fun. "Try This!" outlines an experiment you can investigate.

Guiding Learning

Before Reading
Use a globe or atlas to show students where the Pacific Rim is located. Lead students to discuss what they know about some of the countries and cultures of the region.

During Reading
Key text to guide:

Pages 4–7: Share read these pages. Then have students reread independently and discuss the effects of the movement of the Pacific plate, the different climatic regions, and the varied lifestyles of the people.

Pages 8–11: Remind students to use the glossary. Then say, *Read pages 8 and 10, to find out who first settled the Pacific Islands and why there is now much movement around the Pacific.* When students have finished, discuss their responses. Then read page 9 to students and help them interpret the time line and map. Have them read page 11. Ask, *Do you think Takashi is happy? Why?*

Pages 12–19: Say, *Read to the end of page 19 and find out some of the similarities and differences in four areas of the Pacific Rim.* (Share read with students needing support.) When students have finished, discuss what they've found out. Guide understanding of how natural resources and technology can determine an area's economy.

Pages 20–21: Say, *Read pages 20 and 21 and find out why food is very special to the people of the Pacific Rim.* Discuss the variety of food and the seafood emphasis.

Pages 22–25: Have students read these pages. Then challenge students to discuss some of the different reasons people have told stories. Help them understand the difference between myths and folktales.

Pages 26–27: Say, *Read to the end of page 27 and find out how school life is different around the Pacific Rim.* Ask, *What do nearly all children of the Pacific Rim need to learn?*

Pages 28–29: Read these pages to students. Then explain how to read the map. Probe understanding with questions such as *What does Columbia export to the United States?* (coffee) and *What does Japan import from South Korea?* (TVs)

After Reading
Responding: Challenge students to discuss the similarities and differences in some of the people of the Pacific Rim.

Thinking Activity Master 12
A Yummy Treat: Using Text Organizers and Icons
Reread the recipe on page 20. Discuss the different parts. Then have students write their own recipes, complete with simple icon drawings, for their favorite treats.

www.rigbyinfoquest.com
Zone: People & Places
Link: Pacific Pastimes
Students can research answers on the site:
1. How do people have fun on the Pacific Rim?
2. Which reef on the Pacific Rim is a famous vacation spot?
3. Which city on the Pacific Rim has a large Greek population?
4. What cultural activity is popular on the Pacific Rim?
5. What do the hula and the haka have in common?

Learning Activities
Students can complete activities on the site:
- Work out the Australian lingo.
- Design a travel brochure for a country on the Pacific Rim.

How do people have fun on the Pacific Rim?
Visit www.rigbyinfoquest.com
for more about PACIFIC PASTIMES.

A Yummy Treat

Name _____   Date _____

Write a recipe for a treat. Include icons, or simple pictures, of each of the ingredients. Then sketch the completed treat and list up to four people you would like to share it with.

My yummy treat is _____

Ingredients		Method
•	☐	_____
•	☐	_____
•	☐	_____
•	☐	_____
•	☐	_____
•	☐	_____
•	☐	_____
•	☐	_____

A Picture of My Yummy Treat	I would invite these people to share my treat:
	_____ _____
	_____ _____

Nonfiction Assessment Record

Book Title: *People of the Pacific Rim*

Student _____   Date _____

Say, *Read pages 4 and 5 silently.* Ask, *Why are volcanoes and earthquakes common to this region?*	Did the student understand the influence of the Pacific plate? (Learning Outcome 1)	☐
Say, *Read pages 8 and 10 silently.* Ask, *What was the main reason Europeans explored Southeast Asia?*	Did the student indicate the search for spices or luxury goods? (Purpose for Reading 1)	☐
Ask, *What are some of the reasons for increased movement around the Pacific Rim?*	Could the student recall at least two reasons outlined on page 10? (Learning Outcome 2)	☐
Say, *Read pages 16 and 17 silently.* Ask, *How have the Mapuche been able to preserve their culture?*	Did the student understand the importance of isolation? (Purpose for Reading 2)	☐
Say, *Read pages 20 and 21 silently.* Ask, *Why is seafood important to the people of the Pacific Rim?*	Did the student understand the importance of availability and freshness? (Purpose for Reading 3)	☐
Say, *Read pages 22 through 25 silently.* Ask, *What are two reasons people in the past told stories?*	Did the student mention "passing on culture" and "teaching lessons" or similar reasons? (Learning Outcome 3)	☐
Say, *Look at the map and key on pages 28 and 29.* Ask, *Can you name two countries that import copper from Chile?*	Was the student able to use the map and key to name two of the following countries? Brazil, United States, Japan (Critical Thinking 2)	☐
Ask, *What is the main reason why Japan's economy relies on manufactured goods but Fiji's economy doesn't?*	Did the student understand that Japan lacks natural resources? (Critical Thinking 1)	☐

Student Book Notes—*Shake, Rumble, and Roll*

Synopsis

Shake, Rumble, and Roll explains the origins and effects of volcanoes and earthquakes. The book emphasizes the processes at work just under the Earth's surface. It highlights some historical disasters and provides some useful safety tips.

Vocabulary Development

convection currents, dormant, evacuate, fault, friction, magma, magnitude, Richter scale, state of emergency, subduction, tremor

Challenges in the Text
technical language; scale and map

Cross-Curricular Connections
earth science; health

Learning Outcomes

Students will:
1. be able to explain the causes of earthquakes and volcanoes.
2. recall at least three dangers associated with volcanic eruptions.
3. explain how tsunamis become more intense as they approach a shore.

For Independent Readers

Provide these questions before students read the text:
- Why are there more earthquakes in certain areas of the world?
- How can you prepare for an earthquake?
- How are earthquake strengths measured?
- What causes tidal waves or tsunamis?

Visual Elements

Students have the opportunity to:
1. view a cross-sectional diagram with captions.
2. read sequential captioned diagrams.
3. read and interpret a scale.
4. view double-page spreads.

Purposes for Reading

Possible choices include:
1. to learn about the main effects of earthquakes.
2. to learn about safety issues associated with earthquakes.
3. to learn about some major disasters caused by earthquakes and volcanoes.

Critical Thinking

Students have the opportunity to:
1. form appropriate generalizations about volcanic eruptions.
2. interpret a map to explain the locations of earthquake activity.
3. locate and summarize information in the form of a newspaper article.

Special Features

- Just how destructive can a volcano be? Read "Fast Facts" to find out.
- "In the News" explains what happened when a South American volcano erupted.
- How can you prepare for an earthquake? "In Focus" has the facts.

Guiding Learning
Before Reading
Read the title and explain what the book is about. Ask, *Why do earthquakes and volcanoes happen?* List students' responses for later reference.

During Reading
Key text to guide:

Pages 4–7: Read these pages to students. Discuss the causes of earthquakes and volcanoes. Help students understand and interpret the map on page 6. Ask, *What is the reason for the earthquake zone locations?*

Pages 8–11: Say, *Read to the end of page 11 to find out the locations of earthquakes and the destruction they can cause.* Remind students to refer to the glossary. When students finish, discuss fault lines and the role of plate friction in earthquake creation.

Pages 12–13: Share read. Talk about why shallow water increases the height and power of a tsunami. Ask, *How has science now lowered tsunami disaster risk?*

Pages 14–19: If possible, have students read these pages independently. Then use the diagram to help students understand the chronology of events involved in an eruption. Help students understand that although volcanoes are extremely dangerous, there are usually indications of eruptions well in advance of the events.

Pages 20–25: Say, *Volcanic eruptions can cause death and destruction in several different ways. Read to the end of page 25 and see how many you can discover.* Afterward, discuss the effects of lava, ash, poisonous gases, floods, and mudslides.

Pages 26–27: Have students read the body text on these pages, and discuss the importance of early warning systems. Read "The Richter Scale" to students and be sure that they understand the gradient.

Pages 28–29: Ask, *What can we do to prepare for an earthquake?* After students have had a chance to respond, have them read these pages and compare.

After Reading
Responding: Review students' understanding of why earthquakes and volcanoes happen. Then invite them to state at least two facts they have learned about each of the following: earthquakes, volcanoes, and tsunamis.

Thinking Activity Master 13
On the Scene: Locating and Summarizing Information
Discuss conventions used in newspaper articles, for example, columns, photographs, main points, interviews, and headlines. Have students imagine they are reporting on one of the events from the book and complete a newspaper report with a picture.

www.rigbyinfoquest.com
Zone: Past & Future
Link: Pompeii
Students can research answers on the site:
1. What is archaeology?
2. What happened when Mount Vesuvius erupted in the year 79?
3. What was found at Pompeii?
4. What have archaeologists learned from Pompeii?
5. How did earthquakes affect Pompeii?
6. Were the Pompeii earthquakes the first ones studied?

Learning Activities
Students can complete activities on the site:
- Find the danger zones and the safe spots.
- Test your knowledge of volcanoes.

On the Scene

Name _____   Date _____

1. Choose either a volcanic eruption, an earthquake, or a tsunami. Write an exciting headline about it on the line.
2. Write an article in the two long column boxes. Use the small box at the bottom to draw the photograph you'd like to include.

_____

Nonfiction Assessment Record

Book Title: *Shake, Rumble, and Roll*

Student _____   Date _____

Say, *Read pages 4 and 5 silently.* Ask, *What is the main cause of volcanoes and earthquakes?*	Did the student say "heat" and/or "pressure"? (Learning Outcome 1)	☐
Say, *Read the text and look at the map on page 6.* Ask, *Why are earthquake zones located at the edges of plates?*	Did the student understand the relationship between plate movement and earthquake activity? (Critical Thinking 2)	☐
Say, *Read pages 8 and 9 silently.* Ask, *What are three dangers associated with earthquakes?*	Could the student specify at least three different dangers? (Purpose for Reading 1)	☐
Say, *Read pages 12 and 13 silently.* Ask, *Why do tsunamis get bigger as they approach a shore?*	Did the student understand the effect of shallow water in the growth of the tsunami? (Learning Outcome 3)	☐
Say, *Read pages 15 through 18 silently.* Ask, *Can you explain how lava determines the type of volcanic eruption?*	Could the student use the information from the diagram to form an appropriate generalization? (Critical Thinking 1)	☐
Say, *Read pages 20 through 23 silently.* Ask, *What are three dangers associated with volcanic eruptions?*	Could the student specify at least three different dangers? (Learning Outcome 2)	☐
Say, *Read pages 28 and 29 silently.* Ask, *What are two things that can be done before an earthquake to minimize the risk?*	Did the student indicate securing heavy furniture and making a survival kit? (Purpose for Reading 2)	☐
Ask, *Can you recall at least one earthquake and one volcanic eruption from the book?*	Could the student recall at least one example of each? (Purpose for Reading 3)	☐

Student Book Notes—*Shores of Freedom*

Synopsis

Shores of Freedom explores the main reasons for emigration during the 1600s and the subsequent founding of colonies throughout the world. The book highlights life in the colonies and the events leading up to the American Revolution.

Vocabulary Development
convict, descendant, independence, military, patriotic, penal colony, Pilgrim, plague, Puritan, replica, treaty

Challenges in the Text
historical perspective; biographies

Cross-Curricular Connections
social studies—culture, history

Learning Outcomes

Students will:
1. state the main reasons the Pilgrims left Europe for the New World.
2. display an understanding of how Acadians came to live in Louisiana.
3. be able to explain the significance of Ferdinand Magellan's voyage.

For Independent Readers

Provide these questions before students read the text:
- Why did many people leave Europe to settle in North America?
- What was life like in the colonies?
- What were some of the dangers involved in early sea travel?
- How did the thirteen colonies get their names?

Visual Elements

Students have the opportunity to:
1. read and interpret maps with labels.
2. read a map with captioned text.
3. view photographs and illustrations.
4. view double-page spreads.

Purposes for Reading

Possible choices include:
1. to learn some of the reasons why people chose to travel to new lands.
2. to learn about aspects of life in the original thirteen colonies.
3. to learn about the events leading up to the American Revolution.

Critical Thinking

Students have the opportunity to:
1. compare and contrast colonial life with life in the 21st century.
2. summarize living conditions in Europe during the 1600s.
3. search with the index and contents page to complete a time line.

Special Features

- Find out how Thanksgiving began. "Time Link" has the facts.
- Colonial life was tough. Read "In Focus" and find out just how difficult it was.
- "Profile" explains how a single horse ride in the 1700s is remembered today.
- Check out "Fact Finder" to discover many changes that took place in the late 1700s.

Guiding Learning

Before Reading

Read the synopsis to students. Ask, *Why would people give up their homes to travel to unknown places? What are some of the dangers they would face?* Have students discuss and list their responses.

During Reading

Key text to guide:

Pages 4–5: Share read these pages. Talk about the conditions in Europe, and highlight the importance of Magellan's journey in assuring people they could get back home.

Pages 6–9: Say, *Read to the end of page 9. Find out who the Pilgrims were, why they left England, and what their life was eventually like in the New World.* When students have finished, discuss their responses. Highlight the difficulty of the ocean journey and how the Pilgrims were helped by the local Native Americans.

Pages 10–17: Read pages 10 and 11 to students. Help them read and understand the map. Provide the following guide questions: *What was life like in the early colonies? What jobs did men and women do? How do the lives of colonial children compare to your life today?* Then have students read independently to the end of page 17. When students have finished, have them discuss what they have read.

Pages 18–21: Share read these pages. Discuss the ongoing conflict between the British and French. Ask, *How was the movement of the Acadians different from the movement of other colonists?* (the lack of choice) Point out that there was one positive later result—an exciting cultural mix in Louisiana.

Pages 22–25: Share read these pages. Help students understand the chronology of events and why the colonists fought for independence. Discuss the cartoon on page 24. If appropriate, talk about the use of propaganda in times of conflict.

Pages 26–27: Say, *Read to the end of page 27 and find out how the rest of the world was being colonized during this period.* Discuss what students have found out.

Pages 28–29: Have students read these pages. Challenge students to compare the times with the world today.

After Reading

Responding: Review, revise, and discuss the list composed during the Before Reading session.

Thinking Activity Master 14
Freedom Time Line: Using Parts of a Book to Locate Important Information

Demonstrate searching the index and contents page to locate information. Explain the purpose of the activity, ensuring students understand the instructions. Then have students complete the activity.

www.rigbyinfoquest.com
Zone: Past & Future
Link: Early Colonies

Students can research answers on the site:

1. What was the first permanent English colony in America?
2. Who was Pocahontas?
3. What happened to Jamestown?
4. Can the original Jamestown site be seen today?

Learning Activities

Students can complete activities on the site:

- Try your hand at making a figure from cornhusks.
- Write a letter explaining life as an early settler.

SITESEEING ★ PAST & FUTURE ★

Who was Pocahontas?
Visit www.rigbyinfoquest.com
for more about EARLY COLONIES.

Freedom Time Line

Name _____   Date _____

Use the index and contents page to locate the following events and their dates. Then write each event in the box that contains its correct date.

Treaty of Paris	Champlain founds Quebec	Boston Tea Party
Columbus lands in America	First Thanksgiving	13 colonies established
Magellan's voyage completed	Isaac Newton is born	William Penn dies
Penal colonies in Australia	First colony in Virginia	Paul Revere's ride
Boston Massacre	Mayflower sets sail	

1492	1621	1770
1522	1642	1773
1607	1718	1775
1608	1733	1778
1620	1763	

Nonfiction Assessment Record

Book Title: *Shores of Freedoml*

Student _____ Date _____

Say, *Read pages 4 and 5 silently.* Ask, *What were the conditions in Europe during the 1600s?*	Was the student able to summarize the conditions? (Critical Thinking 2)	☐
Ask, *What were two main reasons people chose to travel to new lands?*	Did the student state "freedom" and "adventure"? (Purpose for Reading 1)	☐
Ask, *Why was Magellan's journey important?*	Did the student understand the significance? (Learning Outcome 3)	☐
Say, *Read pages 6 and 7 silently.* Ask, *Why did the Pilgrims leave England?*	Did the student say "seeking religious freedom" or something similar? (Learning Outcome 1)	☐
Say, *Read pages 12 through 17 silently.* Ask, *How were the roles of women and men different in the early colonies?*	Was the student able to summarize the roles of each gender? (Purpose for Reading 2)	☐
Ask, *How was colonial life for children similar and different from the lives of children today?*	Was the student able to articulate some similarities and differences? (Critical Thinking 1)	☐
Say, *Read pages 20 and 21 silently.* Ask, *What was the main reason Acadians went to settle in Louisiana?*	Did the student understand that the Acadians were forced to leave their homelands? (Learning Outcome 2)	☐
Say, *Read pages 22 and 23 silently.* Ask, *What two events happened in Boston that led to the American Revolution?*	Did the student say "Boston Massacre" and "Boston Tea Party"? (Purpose for Reading 3)	☐

Student Book Notes—*Spice It Up!*

Synopsis

Spice It Up! traces the fascinating history of the search for spices. It explores the importance of the spice trade and highlights some of the more common and exotic spices that are used throughout the world. The book also includes a delicious recipe with easy-to-follow directions.

Vocabulary Development

aroma, bland, circumnavigation, cuisine, condiment, cultivate, currency, Far East, garnish, incense, monopoly, orchid, season, stigma, temperate

Challenges in the Text

historical perspective

Cross-Curricular Connections

social studies; health—food; technology

Learning Outcomes

Students will:

1. be able to state the difference between herbs and spices.
2. display an understanding of the importance of salt.
3. state some of the reasons spices were very important in ancient times.

For Independent Readers

Provide these questions before students read the text:

- How were spices traditionally used?
- What are the main uses of spices in modern times?
- What is allspice? Is it all the spices?
- Why do some cultures use a lot of spices in their meals?

Visual Elements

Students have the opportunity to:

1. read and interpret a range of maps with arrows and keys.
2. view illustrations with labels.
3. read and interpret photographs and illustrations.
4. view double-page spreads.

Purposes for Reading

Possible choices include:

1. to learn how many spices are used throughout the world.
2. to learn the importance of the search for spices in the exploration of the world.
3. to learn about the changing value of several spices.

Critical Thinking

Students have the opportunity to:

1. summarize important information about the uses of chili pepper.
2. form and justify opinions about the spice trade.
3. gather information and use it in the form of a pie graph.

Special Features

- Turn to "Time Link" and find out who first sailed between the Spice Islands.
- Check out a spicy tongue twister. "Word Builder" will have you tongue-tied.
- Some people give spicy wedding gifts. Read all about them in "In Focus."
- Do you want to make a delicious smoothie? "Try This!" has all the instructions.

Guiding Learning

Before Reading

Read the title to students. Ask, *Do you like spicy foods? What are your favorites? How would these foods taste if they didn't contain spices?* Discuss students' responses to these questions.

During Reading

Key text to guide:

Pages 4–5: Read these pages to students. Help them understand both the widespread use of spices and the difference between herbs and spices.

Pages 6–7: Have students read these pages independently. Say, *Find out why spices were important in ancient times.* Ensure students understand the importance in the preservation and flavoring of old meat.

Pages 8–13: Say, *Read to the end of page 13 to find out how the Europeans discovered and fought over spices.* (Share read with students needing support.) When students have finished, discuss the importance of the spice trade to the exploration of Southeast Asia. Ask, *Do you consider the Bugis to be pirates? Why/Why not?*

Pages 14–17: Talk about the importance of chilies in Mexican cooking. Then have students read these pages independently. Talk about the way chili powder made chili meals more accessible to a wider range of people.

Pages 18–23: Say, *Read to the end of page 22 and find out what spices are important to people in other countries.* When students have finished, discuss the values of saffron and vanilla. Ask, *What is the main reason these two spices are expensive?* Read through the recipe on page 23, highlighting the way the text is organized.

Pages 24–27: Say, *Salt and pepper are the most common spices we use. Read to the end of page 27 and find out more about them.* When students have finished, highlight the way salt is produced and processed, and how it is essential to our diet.

Pages 28–29: Read these pages to students. Talk about the longevity and popularity of mustard.

After Reading

Responding: Challenge students to articulate what they have learned about spices from reading this book. Then have them use the index and contents page to substantiate their facts.

Thinking Activity Master 15
Tasty Hot Dogs: Gathering and Using Information

Have each student poll sixteen other students to gather information about mustard and relish use on hot dogs. Review how to display results in the form of a pie graph. Read through the Thinking Activity, and then have students complete the task.

www.rigbyinfoquest.com
Zone: People & Places
Link: Spices

Students can research answers on the site:
1. How do people make curry powder?
2. What are some spices used in sweet treats?
3. What is the source of cinnamon?
4. Which spices can be used as breath fresheners?

Learning Activities

Students can complete activities on the site:
- Test your skill by playing the memory game.
- Choose a spice and make a web about it.

SITESEEING · PEOPLE & PLACES

How do people make curry powder?
Visit **www.rigbyinfoquest.com**
for more about SPICES.

Tasty Hot Dogs

Name _____   Date _____

Part 1: Tasty Hot Dogs

1. Take a poll of 16 students to make a pie graph and to answer Part 2. Keep tallies. First, find out whether they use relish and/or mustard on their hot dogs. You are to use a different color for each choice in the pie graph. Use the same colors in the key.

2. Find out what else they like on their hot dogs. Record totals in the second section of this worksheet. Put the numbers in the brackets.

Key:

Use both mustard and relish	☐
Use mustard but not relish	☐
Use relish but not mustard	☐
Don't use either	☐

Part 2: What else do people like?   Onions (   )   Chilies (   )

Cheese (   )   Ketchup (   )

_____ (   )   _____ (   )

Nonfiction Assessment Record

Book Title: *Spice It Up!*

Student _____   Date _____

Say, *Read pages 4 and 5 silently.* Ask, *What is the main difference between herbs and spices?*	Did the student understand that herbs usually come from the leaves of a plant? (Learning Outcome 1)	☐
Say, *Read pages 6 and 7 silently.* Ask, *What was the main reason why spices were used in ancient times?*	Did the student say preservation or flavoring of old meat? (Learning Outcome 3)	☐
Say, *Read pages 8 through 13 silently.* Ask, *How did the search for spices influence the exploration of the world?*	Did the student understand that much of Southeast Asia was explored and colonized as a result of this search? (Purpose for Reading 2)	☐
Ask, *Do you think the Bagis were pirates? Why/Why not?*	Was the student able to articulate and justify a position? (Critical Thinking 2)	☐
Say, *Read pages 14 and 15 silently.* Ask, *What are some different ways chili pepper can be used?*	Was the student able to summarize information about chili pepper use? (Critical Thinking 1)	☐
Say, *Read pages 20 through 23 silently.* Ask, *Why are saffron and vanilla expensive?*	Did the student understand the expense involved in the production of these spices? (Purpose for Reading 3)	☐
Say, *Read pages 26 and 27 silently.* Ask, *Why is salt highly important in our diets?*	Did the student say it is necessary for life and it helps to flavor bland food? (Learning Outcome 2)	☐
Ask, *Can you recall at least three different spices from three different parts of the world?*	Was the student able to recall the appropriate information from the book? (Purpose for Reading 1)	☐

Student Book Notes—*The Green Scene*

Synopsis

The Green Scene explores the delicate balance in the environment. It outlines the different components of the living world and highlights the roles of plants and animals in the food chain. The book concludes with advice about how we can all contribute to the "green scene."

Vocabulary Development
biodegradable, biodiversity, conserve, mutual, organism, variable
Challenges in the Text
technical vocabulary; food web
Cross-Curricular Connections
earth science; technology; ecology

Learning Outcomes

Students will:

1. be able to explain the tasks of ecologists.
2. recall the main biomes of our planet.
3. understand the importance of symbiotic relationships.

For Independent Readers

Provide these questions before students read the text:

- Why is it important for everyone to help protect the environment?
- What do parasites do?
- What can be done around this school to keep it "green"?
- Are flies necessary or just pests?

Visual Elements

Students have the opportunity to:

1. read and interpret labeled diagrams.
2. read a comparison chart.
3. read and interpret food chain diagrams.
4. view double-page spreads.

Purposes for Reading

Possible choices include:

1. to learn about the nature of ecosystems.
2. to learn how all living things interact in a food chain.
3. to learn some ways our biosphere can be protected.

Critical Thinking

Students have the opportunity to:

1. summarize the differences between populations and communities.
2. interpret a simplified diagram of a food web.
3. research, gather, and organize information about biomes.

Special Features

- Turn to "Try This!" and find out how you can make your own special environment.
- Read about the birth of a baby panda. "In the News" has all the information.
- Check out "In Focus" to discover ecosystems in unlikely places.

Guiding Learning

Before Reading

Read the title and back cover to students. Ask, *Why do you think it is important to learn about different environments? What could you personally do to our area's environment?* Make a list of students' ideas.

During Reading

Key text to guide:

Pages 4–5: Read these pages to students. Discuss the roles of ecologists. Ask, *Why is the work of ecologists important to all of us?*

Pages 6–11: Share read pages 6 and 7. Help students interpret the diagram and understand how these biomes are linked. Either share read or have students read independently to the end of page 11. Highlight the difference between populations and communities. Ask, *Why are controlled environments important?*

Pages 12–13: Say, *Read to the end of page 13 and find out how energy is passed on along a food chain.* Ask, *Are we involved in a food chain? How?*

Pages 14–19: Say, *There are three main tasks carried out by plants and animals in the food chain. Read to the end of page 19 and find out what these are and what each does.* When finished, students can discuss what they have found out. Highlight the relationship between parasites and humans and, if appropriate, give students time to make their own Berlese funnel.

Pages 20–21: Have students read the body text on these pages. Then help students understand the food web flow chart. Ask questions like *What is important to mites? To what are mites important?*

Pages 22–25: Have students read these pages independently. Discuss symbiosis and then how extinction is a natural part of the biosphere.

Pages 26–29: Say, *Read to the end of page 29 and find out what are some of the main dangers to ecosystems. Also find out how we can minimize those dangers.* When students have finished, discuss what they have found out. Challenge them to figure out the food web on pages 28–29. Check answers on page 30.

After Reading

Responding: Invite students to discuss what they have learned from reading this book. Then ask, *How could we as a class help clean up our school area's environment?*

Thinking Activity Master 16
Earth's Biomes: Researching, Gathering, and Organizing Information

Have students research and gather appropriate information about the world's biomes. Then have them organize the information on the worksheet.

www.rigbyinfoquest.com
Zone: Plants & Animals
Link: Ecology

Students can research answers on the site:
1. What is the carbon cycle?
2. What is the greenhouse effect?
3. How is a tapeworm like a mosquito?
4. What is biocontrol?
5. What is ecological succession?

Learning Activities

Students can complete activities on the site:
- Piece together a jigsaw puzzle that shows the six different ways ecologists study Earth.
- Match the pictures and discover some hidden ocean animals.

SITESEEING · PLANTS & ANIMALS

How is a tapeworm like a mosquito?
Visit www.rigbyinfoquest.com
for more about ECOLOGY.

Earth's Biomes

Name _____   Date _____

Research Earth's 5 main biomes. For each biome, find examples of it, the types of plants and animals living there, and the main threats to its life. Organize the information in the chart below.

Biomes	Examples	Plants and Animals	Threats
Aquatic			
Deserts			
Forests			
Grasslands			
Tundra			

Nonfiction Assessment Record

Book Title: *The Green Scene*

Student _____   Date _____

Say, *Read pages 4 and 5 silently.* Ask, *What are the main tasks carried out by ecologists?*	Was the student able to articulate the main tasks? (Learning Outcome 1) ☐
Say, *Read pages 6 and 7 silently.* Ask, *What are the five main biomes on Earth?*	Was the student able to recall all five biomes? (Learning Outcome 2) ☐
Say, *Read pages 8 and 9 silently.* Ask, *In what ways are populations and communities different?*	Did the student understand the main difference between communities and populations? (Critical Thinking 1) ☐
Ask, *What combine to make up an ecosystem?*	Was the student able to summarize information? (Purpose for Reading 1) ☐
Say, *Read pages 12 through 17 silently.* Ask, *What are the different roles of producers, consumers, and decomposers?*	Was the student able to locate the appropriate information and state the roles of each? (Purpose for Reading 2) ☐
Say, *Look at the chart on page 20.* Ask, *What do fungi live on, and what lives on fungi?*	Did the student say fungi live on trees and mites live on fungi? (Critical Thinking 2) ☐
Say, *Read pages 22 and 23 silently.* Ask, *Why are symbiotic relationships important to the life forms living together?*	Did the student display an understanding of mutual advantage? (Learning Outcome 3) ☐
Say, *Read pages 26 and 27 silently.* Ask, *What are three ways we can help our biosphere?*	Was the student able to recall at least three different ways? (Purpose for Reading 3) ☐

Student Book Notes—*The Test of Time*

Synopsis

The Test of Time describes inventions and the stories behind them. The book highlights several inventions that have stood "the test of time" as well as some that didn't catch on. Time lines covering a range of inventions are features of the book.

Vocabulary Development

Industrial Revolution, invention, laser, mass production, millennia, patent, phonograph, prototype, Renaissance, zeppelin

Challenges in the Text
historical perspective

Cross-Curricular Connections
social studies; technology

Learning Outcomes

Students will:

1. be able to state why some inventions have or have not stood the test of time.
2. understand the importance of technology in the creation of new inventions.
3. be able to recall examples of inventions from different time periods.

For Independent Readers

Provide these questions before students read the text:

- What qualities do you think it takes to be a good inventor?
- Which invention could you not do without?
- Some inventions just didn't work. Can you think of any and the reasons for failure?
- What would you invent if you could?

Visual Elements

Students have the opportunity to:

1. gain information from a variety of historical photographs.
2. read and interpret illustrated time lines.
3. read captioned illustrations.
4. view double-page spreads.

Purposes for Reading

Possible choices include:

1. to learn about the development of a range of inventions.
2. to learn about some of the people responsible for inventions.
3. to learn how some inventions acquired their names.

Critical Thinking

Students have the opportunity to:

1. form and justify opinions about the importance of some inventions.
2. sequence and summarize the development of an invention.
3. recognize important information while composing a set of interview questions and possible responses.

Special Features

- Read "Time Link" to discover how clocks, aircraft, and computers have changed.
- It's your turn to be a detective. Check out "Fact Finder" and solve the riddles.
- How could someone combine a hair dryer and popcorn in a new invention? "In Focus" tells you all about it.

Guiding Learning
Before Reading
Discuss the photographs on the cover and title page. Ask, *How has life changed since these photos were taken? Which of these inventions are still around today?*

During Reading
Key text to guide:

Pages 4–5: Read these pages to students. Help them understand why some inventions don't last, and how others come along to replace them. Ask, *How many different ways do you use the wheel?*

Pages 6–11: Show and explain to students the three time lines on these pages. Discuss the meanings of *millennia*, *century*, and *decade*. Then have students read each double-page spread independently. (Share read with students needing support.) When students have finished, challenge them to discuss why the clock has been around much longer than the computer.

Pages 12–13: Using the first example, demonstrate using the grid to solve a riddle. Then have individual students complete the Fact Finder.

Pages 14–19: Say, *Read to the end of page 19 and find out how some famous inventors created what they did.* When students have finished, help them understand how technology has to be in place to create or build an invention.

Pages 20–21: Ask, *How did people entertain themselves before there were televisions or CD-players?* Then have students read these pages and discuss.

Pages 22–23: Say, *Some inventions helped people see things they had never seen before. Can you think of any?* Have students respond, then read, and discuss.

Pages 24–25: Say, *You don't need to be an adult to start inventing. Find out what a 12-year-old girl invented.* Then have students read and discuss.

Pages 26–29: Read the body text on these pages to students. Then challenge them to solve the picture clues on page 27. Read and discuss the unusual inventions on page 29. Ask, *Which of these, if any, do you think will stand the test of time?*

After Reading
Responding: Ask, *Which three inventions from the book do you think are the most important?* Have students justify opinions.

Thinking Activity Master 17
Inventor Interview: Recognizing and Recording Important Information
Demonstrate an appropriate interview (question and answer) format. Tell students that they are to use the index and contents page to find appropriate material about one inventor for writing both questions and answers.

www.rigbyinfoquest.com
Zone: Science & Technology
Link: Space Technology
Students can research answers on the site:
1. How can a rocket fly without fuel?
2. What are space stations?
3. What is the International Space Station?
4. Can an elevator carry objects into outer space?

Learning Activities
Students can complete activities on the site:
- Test your knowledge of technology by answering questions to send the rocket zooming into outer space.
- Explain the ins and outs of some everyday inventions.

How can a rocket fly without fuel? Visit www.rigbyinfoquest.com for more about SPACE TECHNOLOGY.

Inventor Interview

Name _____   Date _____

Choose an inventor from *The Test of Time*. Use the contents page and index to think of four interview questions you would ask the person if you could. Write them and what the inventor might answer.

Inventor: _____

Question 1: _____

Answer: _____

_____

Question 2: _____

Answer: _____

_____

Question 3: _____

Answer: _____

_____

Question 4: _____

Answer: _____

_____

What are three qualities a good inventor should have?

1. _____

2. _____

3. _____

Nonfiction Assessment Record

Book Title: Book Title: *The Test of Time*

Student _____ Date _____

Say, *Read pages 4 and 5 silently.* Ask, *Why didn't some inventions stand the test of time?*	Did the student understand that some inventions replaced others? (Learning Outcome 1)	☐
Say, *Read the time lines on pages 6 through 11 silently.* Ask, *Why wasn't the mechanical clock invented earlier?*	Did the student understand that the technology was not available? (Learning Outcome 2)	☐
Ask, *Can you put the following inventions in the order they were invented? laptop, silicon chip, PC*	Could the student use the time line appropriately? (Critical Thinking 2)	☐
Ask, *In what major way is the development of the clock and computer different?*	Did the student indicate the different time frames and technology bases involved? (Purpose for Reading 1)	☐
Say, *Read pages 15 and 16 silently.* Ask, *In what way was Leonardo da Vinci ahead of his time?*	Could the student provide an appropriate response? (Purpose for Reading 2)	☐
Say, *Read page 26 and 27 silently.* Ask, *What are two different ways inventors name their inventions?*	Could the student list at least two different ways? (Purpose for Reading 3)	☐
Say, *Think about the whole book.* Ask, *Can you remember one invention from 3,000 years ago and one from the late 20th century?*	Could the student recall correct information? (Learning Outcome 3)	☐
Ask, *What do you think is the most important invention presented in this book? Why do you think so?*	Could the student form and justify an opinion? (Critical Thinking 1)	☐

Student Book Notes—*Water Wise*

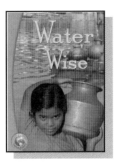

Synopsis

Water Wise highlights the essential nature of water and how its huge demand is becoming increasingly difficult to supply. The book explores water usage around the world and some ways water can be conserved.

Vocabulary Development
dehydrate, evaporation, reservoir, sanitation, transpiration, watershed
Challenges in the Text
poetic language; map interpretation
Cross-Curricular Connections
earth science; social studies; ecology

Learning Outcomes

Students will:

1. be able to state why it is essential that water can change its state.
2. recall at least two ways water can become polluted.
3. display an understanding of how water is supplied to most homes.

For Independent Readers

Provide these questions before students read the text:

- In what different ways is water essential to all life on our planet?
- Why can't we drink ocean water?
- In what ways can we conserve water?
- Why is there rain?

Visual Elements

Students have the opportunity to:

1. view and interpret a pie graph.
2. read a map with an accompanying key.
3. read sequenced diagrams with text.
4. view numbered illustrations with a key.

Purposes for Reading

Possible choices include:

1. to learn about the different forms of water.
2. to learn about the water cycle.
3. to learn about some problems associated with global warming.

Critical Thinking

Students have the opportunity to:

1. use a key to read and interpret a world rainfall map.
2. form and justify opinions about the use of water.
3. gather and then organize information using headings.

Special Features

- Search for different kinds of water by checking out "Fact Finder."
- "In Focus" tells you exactly what happens when you pull the plug.
- Read "Fast Facts" to find out how different people get their water supplies.
- Read "Earth Watch" and discover the terrible effects of water pollution.

Guiding Learning

Before Reading

Have students think about all the different ways they use water. Then ask, *What are some of the ways we can reduce the amount of water we use?* Have students discuss their responses to this question.

During Reading

Key text to guide:
Read the poem and accompanying explanation to students as it occurs.

Pages 4–9: Share read these pages. Pause to help students interpret the diagrams on pages 5 and 7. Ask, *Why is water essential? What different forms does it have?* Highlight the importance of water changing state.

Pages 10–11: Have students read page 10 independently and then discuss. Help students interpret the rainfall map on page 11. Probe with questions like *Can you show me a place that has the most rain?*

Pages 12–15: Ask, *How does clean water get to your home? What happens in places where clean water is not available?* Have students offer ideas and then read these pages independently. Reread the "In Focus" section, ensuring students understand the sequence. Then discuss the main sources of water pollution.

Pages 16–19: Ask, *Besides drinking and washing, how do people use water?* Discuss responses and then have the pages read. Talk about competition for water and simple steps for conserving it.

Pages 20–23: Share read these pages. Help students understand the water cycle on page 21. Then have students discuss the problems associated with global warming.

Pages 24–25: Ask, *Do you think industry has as much right to the use of water as ordinary people do?* Have students read these pages and justify opinions about the use of this dwindling resource.

Pages 26–29: Read page 26 to students and challenge them to use the key to find each of the animals in the ecosystem. Explain pages 28 and 29. Then have students search the illustration, write their answers, and check them on page 30.

After Reading

Responding: Discuss the answers on page 30. Ask, *Do you disagree with anything? Why? Can you think of more wise or wasteful uses that were not included here?*

Thinking Activity Master 18
Water Conservation: Gathering and Organizing Information

Have students think about ways they could conserve water in their homes and at school. Then have them list their ideas under the appropriate headings on the Thinking Activity worksheet. You may wish to assign this for homework. Students can compare their completed answers.

www.rigbyinfoquest.com
Zone: Water, Earth, & Sky
Link: Water

Students can research answers on the site:
1. Why is water important to the human body?
2. How do plants use water?
3. Why can some insects walk on water?
4. What else is notable about water?
5. How is water used in art?
6. How can people have fun with water?

Learning Activities

Students can complete activities on the site:
- Label parts of the water cycle.
- Make a water conservation poster.

SITESEEING · WATER, EARTH, & SKY · **Why can some insects walk on water?** Visit **www.rigbyinfoquest.com** for more about WATER.

Water Conservation

Name _____   Date _____

Write all your ideas about conserving water.

In the Kitchen

_____

_____

_____

_____

In the Bathroom

_____

_____

_____

_____

Water Wise

Outdoors at Home

_____

_____

_____

_____

At School

_____

_____

_____

_____

In Other Places

_____

_____

_____

_____

Nonfiction Assessment Record

Book Title: *Water Wise*

Student _____   Date _____

Say, *Read pages 8 and 9 silently.* Ask, *Can you name three different forms of water?*	Was the student able to name at least three forms? (Purpose for Reading 1) □
Ask, *Why is it essential that water can change its state?*	Did the student understand that without a change of state there could be no rain? (Learning Outcome 1) □
Say, *Look at the map and key on page 11.* Ask, *Can you point to a place that has less than ten inches of rain per year?*	Did the student point to the appropriate area of the map? (Critical Thinking 1) □
Say, *Read pages 12 and 13 silently.* Ask, *What are the steps involved in water getting to our homes?*	Could the student provide an appropriate sequence? (Learning Outcome 3) □
Say, *Read pages 14 and 15 silently.* Ask, *What are two ways water can become polluted?*	Could the student recall two different ways? (Learning Outcome 2) □
Say, *Look at the diagram on page 21.* Ask, *What part does the sun play in the water cycle?*	Did the student understand that the sun causes evaporation? (Purpose for Reading 2) □
Say, *Read pages 22 and 23 silently.* Ask, *Why is global warming becoming a large problem?*	Could the student display a basic understanding of the problem? (Purpose for Reading 3) □
Say, *Read pages 24 and 25 silently.* Ask, *How do you think industry can help conserve water?*	Could the student form and justify an opinion? (Critical Thinking 2) □

Student Book Notes—*What a Century!*

Synopsis

What a Century! presents the major events of the 20th century, one decade at a time. The book highlights the advances made in science, medicine, and technology. It also explores the good times as well as setbacks along the road to the 21st century.

Vocabulary Development
alliance, civil rights, communist, democratic, dictatorship, New Deal, oil crisis, stock market, United Nations
Challenges in the Text
historical perspective
Cross-Curricular Connections
social studies; technology

Learning Outcomes

Students will:
1. be able to state why the 20th century was a time of tremendous change.
2. display an understanding of how life has changed during the last 100 years.
3. discuss challenges facing the planet in the 21st century.

For Independent Readers

Provide these questions before students read the text:
- How has the world changed since your parents or caregivers were your age?
- How have computers changed the world?
- How will the 21st century be different?
- Why do you think people live longer than they did 100 years ago?

Visual Elements

Students have the opportunity to:
1. to gain meaning from historical photographs.
2. read and use information from a game format.
3. read illustrations with captioned text.

Purposes for Reading

Possible choices include:
1. to learn what life was like during different decades of the 20th century.
2. to learn about the reasons for unrest during the 1960s and 1970s.
3. to learn about some of the important discoveries of the 20th century.

Critical Thinking

Students have the opportunity to:
1. compare life in the years directly following the two world wars.
2. form and justify opinions about events of the 20th century.
3. locate and match information with dates in the 20th century.

Special Features

- Read through "My Diary" and discover what life was like during World War II.
- What was the story of the century? Read "In the News" to find out.
- Play a game and learn about the 20th century. "Time Link" is the source.

Guiding Learning
Before Reading
Tell students that this book is about the whole 20th century. Ask, *What were some of the most important events of this century?* Have students record responses to this question for reference after the reading.

During Reading
Key text to guide:

Pages 4–5: Read these pages to students. Discuss the importance of developments, especially in technology, that led to the immense changes from the beginning to the end of the century.

Pages 6–9: Point out the filmstrip inserts that appear on each double-page spread. Then set the following guide questions: *Why can 1901–1910 be called an age of hope? What was different about the war that began in 1914?* Share read these pages and then discuss students' responses to the guide questions. Highlight the terrible conditions faced by soldiers during the first world war.

Pages 10–25: Continue to set similar guide questions for these pages. For example:
Pp. 10–11: *Why were the 1920s enjoyable years?*
Pp. 12–13: *What were two events that made the 1930s a difficult time?*
Pp. 14–15: *How was World War II even worse than World War I?*
Pp. 16–17: *How was life after World War II similar to life after World War I?*
Pp. 18–19: *Which groups of people protested during the 1960s?*
Pp. 20–21: *What two things most concerned people during the 1970s?*
Pp. 22–23: *What was the main problem for developing countries during the 1980s?*
Pp. 24–25: *How did technology change people's lives during the 1990s?*
Have students read independently or, if needed, share read with them. Discuss students' responses and clarify understanding.

Pages 26–29: Read pages 26 and 27 to students. Discuss the challenges for the 21st century. Then explain how to play the game on pages 28–29 and provide playing time.

After Reading
Responding: Review the answers to the question posed in the "Before Reading" session. Then have students use their understanding of the text to add to the list. Ask, *Which three events do you think were the most significant? Why?*

Thinking Activity Master 19
20th Century Events: Locating and Matching Information
Review how to use the contents page, glossary, and index to locate specific information. Discuss the activity, highlighting the example. Then have students complete the activity of matching dates with data.

www.rigbyinfoquest.com
Zone: Art & Entertainment
Link: Entertainment
Students can research answers on the site:
1. What did people enjoy doing in the 1950s?
2. What is a fad?
3. When were hula hoops invented?
4. When did the yo-yo become popular?

Learning Activities
Students can complete activities on the site:
- Travel through the twentieth century as you play the "Game of the Century."
- Create a new fad toy.

What did people enjoy doing in the 1950s?
Visit www.rigbyinfoquest.com
for more about ENTERTAINMENT.

20th Century Events

Name _____   Date _____

Draw a line to match each decade with an event.

Decade	Event
1901–1910	The United Nations is set up to try preventing future wars.
1911–1920	The Berlin Wall finally comes down.
1921–1930	The first totally computer-animated movie is made.
1931–1940	Adolf Hitler gains power in Germany.
1941–1950	Henry Ford invents the first mass-produced automobile.
1951–1960	The first communist state is created.
1961–1970	Elvis Presley takes the world by storm.
1971–1980	Alexander Fleming discovers penicillin.
1981–1990	Neil Armstrong becomes the first person to walk on the moon.
1991–2000	Punk rock expresses the feelings of some young people.

Thinking Activity Master 19: Locating and Matching Information—What a Century!

114

Nonfiction Assessment Record

Book Title: *What a Century!*

Student _____   Date _____

Say, *Read pages 4 and 5 silently.* Ask, *What is the main reason people are now better off than 100 years ago?*	Did the student understand the importance of the advances made, especially in technology? (Learning Outcome 1) ☐
Ask, *How is your life different than it would have been 100 years ago?*	Did the student display an understanding of the major changes? (Learning Outcome 2) ☐
Say, *Read pages 10 through 11 and 16 through 17 silently.* Ask, *How was life similar during these two decades?*	Did the student understand the need for a positive outlook following the hardship of the war years? (Critical Thinking 1) ☐
Say, *Read pages 18 through 19 silently.* Ask, *What were two reasons people protested during this decade?*	Did the student say "civil rights," "women's rights," and/or "the Vietnam War"? (Purpose for Reading 2) ☐
Ask, *Do you think it was worth all the money it took to land a person on the moon?*	Could the student offer and justify a consistent opinion? (Critical Thinking 2) ☐
Say, *Read pages 26 and 27 silently.* Ask, *Can you name two challenges facing the world in the 21st century?*	Did the student offer two appropriate challenges? (Learning Outcome 3) ☐
Say, *Think about the whole book.* Ask, *Which decade would you have liked to grow up in? Why?*	Could the student use text information in the response? (Purpose for Reading 1) ☐
Ask, *Which three inventions or discoveries of the 20th century do you think were the most important? Why?*	Could the student recall three important inventions or discoveries? (Purpose for Reading 3) ☐

Student Book Notes—*Wild Planet*

Synopsis

Wild Planet highlights the delicate balance in different ecosystems and presents the natural and introduced threats to some species. The book explores some of the organized efforts being made to save endangered animals and how anyone can help.

Vocabulary Development
adapt, alien, Earth Summit, ecosystem, endangered, exotic, habitat, poach, refuge

Challenges in the Text
technical language; diary format

Cross-Curricular Connections
life sciences

Learning Outcomes

Students will:

1. state two reasons why some animal species become endangered.
2. display an understanding of the problems associated with introduced species.
3. state several ways people can help endangered animals.

For Independent Readers

Provide these questions before students read the text:

- What does *endangered* mean?
- Which plants and animals do you know are endangered?
- Why is it important to save endangered animals? What could you do to help?

Visual Elements

Students have the opportunity to:

1. view a variety of images.
2. read and interpret maps with captions.
3. read text with bulleted points.
4. read text in diary format.

Purposes for Reading

Possible choices include:

1. to learn about the natures and importance of ecosystems.
2. to learn about some ways plants and animals adapt.
3. to learn about efforts being made to save endangered animals.

Critical Thinking

Students have the opportunity to:

1. form and justify opinions about land use.
2. form generalizations about food chains.
3. summarize information in a KWL chart.

Special Features

- Check out "In Focus" and discover a new threat to sea otters.
- Read about the problem of cane toads in "What's Your Opinion?"
- How do tiger cubs live? Turn to "My Diary" for a peek.
- You can make a real difference. Find out how by reading "Earth Watch."

Guiding Learning

Before Reading

Provide copies of Thinking Activity Master 20. Discuss the KWL chart and have students begin to fill the first two columns. Students should continue to add to the chart as they read the book.

During Reading

Key text to guide:

Pages 4–5: Share read these pages and highlight the reasons wildlife can become endangered. Help students read and interpret the captioned map.

Pages 6–11: Remind students to use the glossary. Then say, *Read to the end of page 10 to find out why ecosystems are important and some of the problems they face.* (Share read with students needing support.) When students have finished, discuss ecosystems and the problem of introduced species. Highlight the delicate balance in food chains. Read page 11 to students, and then challenge them to form and justify their own opinions.

Pages 12–13: Ask, *What would be the main problem for flightless birds?* Have students read these pages and respond. Highlight the problem of introducing foreign species into a tightly controlled ecosystem.

Pages 14–17: If possible, have students read these pages independently. Highlight the care and attention given by Toba to her cubs. Ask, *Why do you think the tiger has become a symbol of conservation efforts?*

Pages 18–23: Say, *What different things do people do to help save endangered animals? Read to the end of page 23 and find out.* When students have finished, discuss the range of strategies used to save animals.

Pages 24–25: Share read these pages and invite students to offer and justify their opinions on land use.

Pages 26–27: Say, *Read to the end of page 27 and find out what is being done to help the wolves in Canada.* When students have finished, discuss the success of this project.

Pages 28–29: Ask, *How can ordinary people, including children, help save endangered wildlife?* Have students respond and then read these pages.

After Reading

Responding: Have students think about and list what they can do to help save endangered wildlife.

Thinking Activity Master 20
KWL Chart: Summarizing Information

Have students review the information they have included in their KWL charts. Have students use the book to complete as much of the final column as possible. Discuss resources (including *Rigby InfoQuest* Siteseeing) that could be used to answer any remaining questions.

www.rigbyinfoquest.com
Zone: Plants & Animals
Link: Endangered Animals

Students can research answers on the site:

1. What is an endangered species?
2. Why is the giant panda endangered?
3. Why are some frogs endangered?
4. Where are Hamilton's frogs found?
5. Where are ring-tailed lemurs found?
6. Are polar bears endangered?

Learning Activities

Students can complete activities on the site:

- Set up an interview to find out your classmate's opinions.
- Explore the coral reefs and collect data like a biologist.

Why are some frogs endangered?
Visit www.rigbyinfoquest.com
for more about ENDANGERED ANIMALS.

KWL Chart

Name _____   Date _____

Fill in the KWL chart before, during, and after you read *Wild Planet*.

What I **Know** About Endangered Animals	What I **Want** to Know About Endangered Animals	What I **Learned** About Endangered Animals

Nonfiction Assessment Record

Book Title: *Wild Planet*

Student _____   Date _____

Say, *Read pages 4 and 5 silently.* Ask, *What are the two main reasons some species become endangered?*	Did the student indicate "people" and "natural causes"? (Learning Outcome 1) ☐
Say, *Read pages 6 and 7 silently.* Ask, *Why is it important to maintain ecosystems?*	Did the student understand that plants and animals depend on one another? (Purpose for Reading 1) ☐
Ask, *What happens if a food chain is disturbed?*	Could the student form an appropriate generalization? (Critical Thinking 2) ☐
Say, *Read pages 10 and 11 silently.* Ask, *Why are introduced, or "alien," species a problem?*	Did the student understand the harmful effects of introduced species? (Learning Outcome 2) ☐
Say, *Read pages 12 and 13 silently.* Ask, *How did New Zealand birds adapt because they had no predators?*	Did the student understand that this was the reason they became flightless? (Purpose for Reading 2) ☐
Say, *Read page 25 silently.* Ask, *What do you think about the problems facing farmers? Why?*	Could the student form and justify an appropriate opinion? (Critical Thinking 1) ☐
Say, *Think about the whole book.* Ask, *What are three different ways people are trying to save endangered animals?*	Did the student offer at least three examples from the book? (Purpose for Reading 3) ☐
Ask, *What are at least two ways you can help endangered species?*	Could the student recall at least two examples from the book? (Learning Outcome 3) ☐

Index